A *Student Guide to*
College Composition

by
William Murdick

JAIN PUBLISHING COMPANY
Fremont, California

jainpub.com

Jain Publishing Company, Inc. is a diversified publisher of college textbooks and supplements, as well as professional and scholarly references, and books for the general reader. A complete, up-to-date listing of all the books, with cover images, descriptions, review excerpts, specifications and prices is always available on-line at **jainpub.com**. Our booksPLUS® division provides custom publishing and related services in print as well as electronic formats, and our learn24x7® division offers electronic course and training materials development services.

Library of Congress Cataloging-in-Publication Data

Murdick, William.
   A student guide to college composition / by William Murdick.
     p. cm.
  Includes bibliographical references and index.
   ISBN 0-87573-100-7 (Paperback : alk. paper)
    1. English language—Rhetoric—Handbooks, manuals, etc.
  2. Report writing—Handbooks, manuals, etc. I. Title.

PE1408.M786 2003
808'.042—dc21

2003000874

A Student Guide to
College Composition

Contents

PART I   Succeeding in Composition

PART II   Meeting the Challenges of Academic Writing

PART III   Handling the Major Assignments

List of Illustrations

About This Book

A Student Guide to College Composition is a college textbook meant to serve as the main rhetoric for a Composition I course. However, because composition programs vary considerably, the book might be appropriate for any course in a composition sequence. It can even function as a supplementary text for the whole program. *A Student Guide* would normally be used in conjunction with a reader and a handbook.

Unique Character

A Student Guide to College Composition is a unique textbook in several ways. First, it talks directly to students, using the intimate second person point of view. The voice of the author is like that of a favorite uncle who happens to be a college English professor, talking to a niece or nephew who is going off to college. As would be likely in that situation, the book touches on non-writing as well as writing issues that bear on success in composition and in college.

Traditional composition textbooks are "topic oriented." They start with a standard list of topics and then methodically address each one, usually quite briefly. This book is "task oriented." It shows students how to write the specific kinds of short essays that comprise the main assignments in a contemporary composition course.

As a background to that, instead of covering many topics quickly, it discusses at length three of the most difficult challenges for first-year student writers: fully developing points, reasoning like an educated adult, and incorporating the words of other writers into one's own text. If students can improve their handling of those three challenges, the quality of their essays should improve noticeably.

Finally, *A Student Guide to College Composition* recognizes the growing presence of the timed writing test in composition programs, as a placement device and an exit hurdle. The appendix presents an extensive guide to passing such tests.

Structure and Content

Part 1: Succeeding in Composition describes contemporary composition programs, orienting students to what lies ahead. **Chapter 1** tells students what they need to know about their own program and course, and how to get that information. **Chapter 2** discusses eighteen do's and don'ts for becoming a competent, successful student.

Part 2: Meeting the Challenges of Academic Writing focuses on three important aspects of academic prose that are particularly difficult for first-year students.

(1) Many first-year writers don't know how to develop their main points adequately enough to achieve their goals as writers. They say too little to get the job done. **Chapter 3** contrasts thin and thick development, and it provides concrete methods for achieving the latter.

(2) Some beginning student writers project a voice that is too loud or insistent or informal. They exaggerate or fail to qualify statements adequately. They are loose with facts and figures. Their arguments lack fairness and civility. **Chapter 4** describes the "educated voice" and discusses the reasoning, attitudes, and practices that underlie it.

(3) As composition programs gravitate more toward writing in response to reading, the ability to incorporate outside sources becomes important in all composition courses, not just the traditional research paper course. **Chapter 5** shows students when to bring in outside voices, how to format such inclusions, and how to document sources to avoid plagiarism.

Part 3: Handling the Major Assignments offers doable approaches to the five most common essay assignments. **Chapters 6-10** address the personal narrative, the informative article, the argument on a controversial issue, the literary criticism essay, and the long research paper. For each type of essay, the book provides possible structures and directions for development, as well as other guidance. In this section, the book takes a very practical how-to approach.

The appendix, **How to Pass a Timed Writing Test**, explains the purposes of such tests, the kinds of prompts used today, how to analyze a prompt, how to organize an essay response, how to recognize and eliminate fatal signs of incompetence, how to inject signs of intelligence, and what to do in the event of failure.

Credit Due

This book was significantly improved thanks to the efforts of **Monica Bomengen**, a member of the Jain Publishing Company advisory board for this book, who submitted a very useful, comprehensive critique, and **Yoshiko Murdick**, who proofread the text and produced the art work.

The excerpt pp. 19-20 by Traci E. Augustosky from *Comp Tales*, edited by Richard H. Haswell and Min-Zhan Lu, was printed with permission of Pearson Education, Inc., Glenview, Il.

The poem "The Hound" by Robert Francis was printed with permission of the University of Massachusetts Press, Amherst.

Part I

Succeeding in Composition

Most student failure in composition results from ineffective behavior, not hopelessly poor writing ability. The chapters in this section show you how to be a good student.

1

Understanding Composition

Millions of students in the U.S. enroll in a composition course each year. Welcome to a big club. And an old one. U.S. colleges have been teaching composition ever since Harvard University, in 1874, decided to give a writing test to its applicants. A majority of them flunked it. The dons of Harvard were shocked to discover that 20-year-old prep school graduates didn't write like "little professors."

Out of this dismay grew the idea for the college composition course to help students acquire the basic skills of writing they had supposedly failed to learn in high school. Eventually, however, English professors began to understand that academic writing is a difficult intellectual enterprise and that it doesn't make sense to think that first-year students are going to be particularly good at it. From this new realization has come the full-blown composition program, of the kind you will likely encounter if you are entering college today.

This chapter provides a quick overview of contemporary composition. Succeeding in composition begins with understanding your local program and courses.

1-1 Composition Programs

The most typical college program consists of three courses:

1) a pre-composition or basic writing course for weak writers
2) the regular essay writing course

3) a second essay writing course that includes the writing of a long research paper.

Expect to take a placement test so that the school can determine which course you should start with—a preparatory course or the first regular writing course. Placement tests nowadays usually take the form of timed essays. Along with fellow students, you show up at an auditorium or a large classroom on campus, or some designated place off campus, and there you are given a prompt, an examination book to write in, and from one to two hours to write an essay in response to the prompt.

You may also have to pass a similar writing test, this time called an "exit test," in order to achieve sophomore or junior year status, or to graduate from the college. You will probably be allowed to take the exit test more than once, and you may be able to start taking the test in your freshman year and continue to take it each semester until you pass. You would be wise to find out, as soon as possible, what your program requires and allows.

The appendix at the back of this book discusses how to write an effective essay on a timed test. If you find yourself having to take one of these exams, take the trouble to read that appendix and practice writing a timed essay. Practicing an effective approach, such as the one described in the appendix, will almost certainly improve your performance. Failing a timed writing test can disrupt your smooth progress through college.

The three-course program is common, but other versions of composition abound. Some schools offer only one composition course, and others, on the quarter system, as many as five or six. Make sure you understand how the program at your school is designed. Here are some possible sources of information:

- The college catalogue, available from the admissions office or online at the school's Web site, will offer some information under "course descriptions."

- The English departmental Web site might describe the program.
- Freshman orientation may provide information or an opportunity to ask questions.
- The English Department may publish a pamphlet or a handout describing the program, which you can pick up in the English office.
- As a last resort, the English secretary, or the director of composition, or the English department chair will be able to answer your questions. Get on the phone or go to the department in person.

Here is some of the information you should know about your school's composition program and about the specific course you are taking, ideally before the first day of classes:

1. How the testing system works
2. How many courses you will have to take, as a result of your score on the placement test (once you have taken it)
3. The general content of each course in the series you will have to take
4. The required textbooks for your first course (check in the campus bookstore)
5. The location of the classroom, so you're not late to class on the first day.

If you are new to the campus, obtain a campus map from the admissions office or print one from the school's Web site, and then a day or two before classes begin, take a tour of the campus to locate the rooms where each of your classes will meet. Rooms are usually easy to locate in modern buildings, but old buildings often have classrooms that are tucked away in obscure corners or hidden up back stairways.

On the first day of composition class, your instructor will probably distribute one or more printed handouts describing the course in detail, as this particular instructor teaches it, and possibly providing information about how to contact your instructor by phone or e-mail. Although written handouts are the normal way this information is distributed, the instructor may present some important information about the course orally as a lecture at the beginning of the class, which is why you don't want to be late for this first meeting. Bring a notebook and take notes.

1-2 Types of Courses and Teacher Expectations

What your composition teacher will expect from you will depend mainly on what kind of composition (or pre-composition) course you are in. Below is a description of the most common types of courses and what you will be expected to do in them. You can get clues to your course type from the course title, the textbooks you have purchased, the school's course catalogue, and the handouts your instructor gives you on the first day of class, as well as anything your instructor says about the course.

Some of the courses described below that are labeled "pre-composition" may show up as a component in the first regular essay writing course, so take a look at them even if you are going to be starting with the first regular course.

The Grammar and Sentence Correctness Course

In this pre-composition course, you will study a grammar workbook that has essentially the same content as the text you used in 7th grade. (You'll probably find the subject matter just as ornery today as it was then.) Besides grammar, your workbook will include information on a limited set of common sentence errors, such as a breakdown of subject-verb agreement, punctuation faults, and improper word usage. You will fill in exercises for homework and take regular quizzes and tests.

The best strategies for this course are to:

1. Read the short chapters more than once; you will often find that after re-reading difficult material several times, it begins to sink in
2. Buy, or check out of the library, another grammar/sentence-correctness workbook and use it to obtain an alternative explanation of each point
3. Study outside of class in pairs or groups; it's more fun and you'll learn from your interaction with fellow students as you try to puzzle things out together
4. Use the writing center as needed (writing centers are discussed in the next chapter).

Although working with other students is a good idea, don't let others simply do the homework for you. Your grade will depend mostly on how well you do on quizzes and tests, not on how perfect your homework is. It's better to struggle during the homework stage, and learn, than to struggle during the tests, and flunk.

The Sentence and Paragraph Writing Course

In this pre-composition course, the focus will be on learning how to write complicated and correct sentences. The course will cover much of the information taught in the grammar course described above. However, it will also include sentence combining and possibly other types of exercises that require you to write sentences of one type or another.

In sentence combining, the instructor provides you with a short set of sentences and then asks you to combine them into one. You may be allowed to combine the sentences any way you wish, an activity called "free combining." You shouldn't have much trouble if you are a native speaker of English. Just read your final combined sentences aloud to make sure they sound like English.

However, you may be asked to combine sentences in specified ways. For example:

> Combine these three sentences. Make the first an adverb clause and the last a participial phrase.
>
> —He wanted to buy an unusual bread for dinner.
> —He went into Brooklyn.
> —He searched for an exotic loaf in the ethnic neighborhoods.

You could write this sentence for an answer:

> Because he wanted to buy an unusual bread for dinner, he went into Brooklyn, searching for an exotic loaf in the ethnic neighborhoods.

If the structures to be used are specified, as in the example above, you will have to deal with the grammar problem. Use your textbook to find examples and explanations of the specified structures, such as "adverb clause" and "participial phrase." If you're having trouble, use the writing center and work in pairs or groups.

If your instructor is expecting you to write specified structures, you will have to learn the grammatical terminology for about a dozen different phrases and clauses. For example, you will have to learn what an adverb clause consists of, or looks like, so that you can produce one on the tests. One approach is to memorize short simple versions of each structure that you can call to mind during a test. These will remind you of what the structures look like. For *adverb clause*, you might learn: <u>Because he likes adverb clauses</u>, John writes millions of them / <u>If he likes adverb clauses</u>, does that mean that he likes adverbs? / He writes adverb clauses furiously <u>when he is in the mood for them</u>. The underlined structures are adverb clauses. Usually, the more idiotic the statements, the easier they are to remember. Always use the grammatical term in the sentence. For *infinitive* (*to* plus a verb), this one sentence will do: She wanted <u>to write</u> infinitives in order <u>to achieve</u> infinite happiness.

Sometimes the sentence writing course is expanded to include paragraph writing, in which case you will learn how to compose a certain kind of paragraph that can stand alone as a mini-essay. Such paragraphs are said to have "organic unity." They are described in the next section.

The Pre-Structured Essay Course

In this course, you will write very short essays—one or two pages of double-spaced, word processed text. Importantly, the essays will all have the same structure:

An introductory paragraph beginning with, or leading to, a thesis sentence. The thesis sentence states the one main point of the essay.

Generally two to four paragraphs in the body of the essay, all of which have "organic unity." An organic paragraph begins with a topic sentence that says something about the thesis of the essay. The rest of the paragraph talks only about the topic sentence. This restriction on content is what gives the paragraph its "unity."

A conclusion that repeats the thesis and often summarizes the main supporting points.

Box 1-1 provides an example of this kind of essay. In that model, the thesis is: "In fact, they are quite different." The topic sentences appear at the beginning of each paragraph in the body of the essay. The first topic sentence, for example, is: "The one-handed backhand is a true backhand shot, but the two-hander is not."

In this type of composition class, *organization is paramount.* Writing the pre-structured essay is fairly easy, provided you understand the shape of the structure and follow these simple guidelines: Make each topic sentence relevant to the thesis, and then within each paragraph, discuss only the topic sentence and don't veer off onto other topics.

Box 1-1 A Pre-Structured Essay (or "Five-Paragraph Theme")

Note: The thesis sentence and the developing topic sentences are printed in bold.

The Two Backhands

Since the 1970s, the two-handed backhand has become very popular in tennis. In recent years, you may have seen Andre Agassi pounding two-handers for winners on his way to becoming Wimbledon champ. On the other hand, you may have also seen Pete Sampras blasting traditional one-handed backhands on his way to winning the U.S. Open. Both shots are still current among the greatest players. This doesn't mean that they are essentially the same shot. **In fact, they are quite different.** ←[thesis sentence]

The one-handed backhand is a true backhand shot, but the two-hander is not. A player like Sampras, in executing the one-handed shot, will turn his back to the approaching ball and swing backwards toward the net with his right arm. For Agassi, however, the backhand is actually a left-handed forehand, powered by the left arm and wrist. Because Agassi, like most right-handed players, has never learned to hit a one-armed left-handed forehand shot, he uses his right arm and hand to steady the racket. If Agassi's right hand weren't stabilizing the forward motion of the racket, the racket head would wobble, making the shot impossible.

The shots are different also in terms of how the players position themselves for executing the stroke. Sampras hits the ball further away from his body than Agassi does. Keeping both hands on the racket reduces the distance Agassi can stretch the racket away from his body. Sampras gets his back to the ball at the outset of the motion and Agassi stands sideways, or even faces slightly open toward the oncoming ball.

Finally, the follow through for the top spin shot is different for each player. Sampras stays down through the shot, keeping his knees bent. Agassi rises up. Sampras finishes with the racket head high, pointing to the sky. Agassi follows through by twisting his body to the right and swinging the racket fully over his right shoulder.

Although these shots are both called "backhands," they are significantly different. Yet both are used by professionals today to effectively handle baseline shots.

The Romantic Rhetoric Course

The romantic rhetoric course asks students to discard the academic style and seek an "authentic voice." You will write essays about your personal experiences in your own natural (though grammatical) voice, avoiding stiff academic prose.

Often, the more personal and confessional your essays are, the more interesting and well written they will be, and the better your instructor will like them. However, don't get too confessional and start talking about the paper you wrote for another student in the class or the stash of weed you keep in your dorm room closet. Instructors cannot ignore unethical or illegal acts.

If you find yourself in this type of course, take a long hard look at Chapter 6 in this book, which talks about writing personal narratives.

The Modern Course

The latest version of composition does not require you to fit your essay into a pre-structured format or to avoid academic prose. Instead, your instructor will want you to focus on taking into account the reader's needs as well as your own purposes in writing. For example, if you are writing an informative essay whose purpose is to educate your readers in a general way about some subject (such as how the stock market works), your instructor will be measuring your essay according to how well you achieve that purpose and how well you take into account what your readers need to be told in order to understand your points. If writing a persuasive essay on a controversial issue, your instructor will expect you, among other things, to anticipate a reader's objections to your points and to speak to those objections.

To write a good essay, then, you must pursue a clear purpose and keep your eye on the reader. You should be focused on meaning, not any kind of fixed structure, such as a paragraph consisting of a topic sentence followed by concrete supporting detail. You may in fact write such a paragraph

at some point in the essay, but not deliberately or con-
sciously. Your conscious mind will be turned toward developing content to achieve your purpose. This approach is based
on research into how professional writers think and work.

For purposes of learning, the modern course requires
you to use a "collaborative, multi-draft writing process."
Collaborative means that you critique other students' work
and you get critiques from your fellow students and from the
instructor. Multi-draft means that you develop your essay
through revisions based on these critiques.

Your instructor will expect you to take these critiques
seriously and to make major changes and improvements as
you revise. You may have to turn in all versions of each paper
so that the instructor can evaluate you on how well you have
used the revision process to improve your text. If so, *save
everything!* Don't throw out any of your notes, outlines, or
early drafts of papers. Every time you open a file on your computer to begin revising a paper, immediately use the "save as"
function to save the file under a new name, representing a
new draft (for example, 2ndpaper4 for the second paper,
fourth draft). Then type in this new filename and the date at
the top of the paper—2ndpaper4/Oct 7—so that the printed
copy of each draft will be identifiable.

To advance the multi-draft approach, your instructor
may use portfolio assessment. Under this system, you will not
turn in individual papers for grading, but will turn in a set of
papers, usually at the middle and end of the term, and you
will receive one grade for each set or portfolio. This allows
you to continue working on individual papers, revising them,
until the portfolio is due. You should take advantage of portfolio assessment by occasionally reading over each "finished"
paper to see how it sounds. Is it smoothly written and well-
developed? Does the voice coming through sound mature
and intelligent? If not, revise again to improve the essay.

Modern courses often require you to read and respond
to professionally written essays, and one of your textbooks
may be an anthology of such work. Chapter 5 in this book will

help you incorporate the words and ideas of other authors into your text. Part 3 discusses the various kinds of essays students are asked to write in modern courses.

1-3 The Computer Component

Many colleges now maintain computer labs reserved for composition classes. You may find yourself working in a networked computer classroom which your instructor has established for your class, one which allows you to electronically

- receive instructions and assignments from the instructor
- make your texts available to the instructor for comment and grading
- make your texts available to other students for comment
- comment on the work of other students
- participate in discussions of course work with members of your writing group or with anyone else in the class.

Although the computer lab will be reserved, at least for certain hours, for composition classes, you probably won't have to be in the lab to carry out any of the above activities. You should be able to access the composition-course network from other labs on campus, and even from your dorm room or home, provided you have a computer online.

In fact, you may be able to enroll in a composition class which rarely or never meets, except electronically through Web sites and e-mail communication. Online courses are useful to people with heavy work schedules, and they work well for students who are independent by nature and comfortable with computers. However, many other students who have ended up in such courses report that they don't like them. The average student, apparently, misses the face-to-face human contact of the conventional class. If you think you belong to that last category, avoid online courses.

1-4 Support Services

Your college very likely has a writing center, a tutoring facility for students having trouble with a writing assignment or grammar homework. The next chapter discusses in detail when and how to use your school's writing center.

All colleges these days provide support services for handicapped students and students with learning disabilities, including assistance with composition classes. If you are qualified for such services, or think you may be, find out what is available and how qualification is determined. To learn about such matters, walk into the nearest administration building and up to the first counter you see and ask. You'll be sent to the right place. Or you can phone the school's main number. The campus operators will know where to route your call.

1-5 Awards for Excellence

Many composition programs exempt talented students from composition courses, usually on the basis of their place-ment essays. If you are a good writer, you may be excused from one or more composition course requirements.

Many modern programs offer awards for the best essays written in the regular composition courses. If you think you might be able to win one of those prizes, ask your instructor about getting one of your compositions submitted for consid-eration. Winning such an award, or even being nominated (having your essay submitted by the teacher), looks good on your resume.

1-6 Survival

You may have gotten the impression from this first chap-ter that you are responsible for finding out a lot of things about your college in general and composition in particular. That's correct. Even small colleges are big bureaucracies, and information is not always distributed effectively. You have to seek it out. No one is going to tap you on the shoulder and tell you what you need to know at every step.

You may be part of a huge campus community, but in a sense you're also on your own. Be aggressive about seeking information—and about learning, too. In college, you have to take control of your own academic career.

2

Doing What Works

Even if you are a weak writer, you should be able to pass your composition courses with decent grades. This chapter provides *do*'s and *don't*'s for succeeding in composition. Your job is to get serious, make the effort, and do what works.

2-1 Buy Your Textbooks Early

Once you know which composition course you will be taking, purchase the textbooks as soon as possible. The campus or town bookstores order textbooks on the basis of early enrollment figures, which can be inaccurate. They often under-order, because they'd rather "special order" a few copies later for desperate students than deal with unsold copies. Instructors will not delay giving reading assignments just because the stores have run out of books and you are waiting for the text to come in.

If you know your instructor's name and the official course title, you can find the correct books in the bookstore before classes begin. At some schools, you don't even need to know who your instructor will be because all instructors are required to use the same composition textbooks.

You can save money by purchasing your textbooks cheaply through Internet bookstores, using a credit card, but make sure that you order the correct edition of each book. For example, if your class has been assigned the *MLA Handbook for Writers of Research Papers, Fifth Edition,* don't buy the fourth edition of that book. Internet stores don't always carry the latest editions. Expect to wait ten days to receive your texts in the mail. You can find the best prices using this Web site: **www.bestbookbuys.com**.

2-2 Become Computer Competent

Many composition instructors today require students to submit word processed texts. If you don't like computers, you need to get past that aversion. Computers are a great boon to writers as basic tools, and Internet research is becoming a standard part of college work. Box 2-1 lists word processing functions you should know. Check off the ones you have control over already, so you can see what remains to be learned.

Box 2-1 Check List of Word Processing Functions for College Writing

---

To meet specifications for composition manuscripts:
___line spacing
___font size
___margins
___headers and footers, including page numbering options
___font style (esp. italics and underlining)
___text centering
___regular indentation (for long quotations) and hanging indentation (for bibliographies)

To achieve efficiency:
___spell check, word count, thesaurus, and dictionary
___printing options (esp. print preview and print multiple copies)
___save options, especially saving to a backup disk and saving your file under another name (like paper2ver4)
___cut and paste
___find and replace
___footnotes
___auto-correct of typing errors
___auto-numbering of lists
___templates and macros
___working with multiple files; inserting one file into another
___graphics creation and insertion
___table creation and insertion

Becoming proficient with word processing is something you will probably have to do on your own. Don't expect your composition teacher to conduct a mini-course on the subject. If you've been using WordPerfect on a Macintosh at home and the college lab uses Word on a Windows platform, buy or check out of the library a beginner's book on Word for Windows and spend a couple of Saturday mornings examining the program. These programs come with built-in help menus which can also be used to learn the basics. If you get completely lost, the student in charge of the computer lab will probably be able to help you. Don't be afraid to ask.

To really succeed in college, you have to be aggressive about learning.

2-3 Attend Class

Some students can get away with freely cutting certain types of classes, but composition is not one of them. Too much important work is done in the classroom. Missing class accounts for more instances of grade reduction and outright failure than any other kind of incompetent student behavior.

Pay close attention to your instructor's attendance policy. You will probably be allowed to miss a certain number of classes with impunity. After that, grade penalties start to kick in. Once you have used up your "free cuts," don't expect to be allowed additional absences just because you have an "excuse." Save your allowed cuts for those times when illness or mishap or emergency prevents you from attending class. That's what those cuts are for. They are not an allotment of vacation days.

What to Do If You Have Missed a Class
When you do miss a class, call one of your classmates to find out what you missed and whether any assignment was made for the next class meeting. Make sure you have a contact person in each class, just for this purpose.

In high school, if you miss a day, you can get away with not turning in work when you return to class, because you weren't there to get the assignments. Not so in college. You're responsible for finding out what's due. If you can't get through to your contact person, call or e-mail the instructor. On the first day of class, most instructors hand out information sheets about the course which include their phone number or e-mail address. Find a place in your study room to keep those sheets for all your classes so you don't lose them. Often instructors' e-mail addresses and even phone numbers can be found on departmental Web sites, which will be accessible through your school's main Web site.

What to Do If You Know You Are Going to Miss a Class

If you know in advance that you are going to miss a class, go to the instructor and ask about the work that you'll miss and the assignments that are coming up. Also, submit in advance any work that will be due on the day of your absence, or arrange with the instructor to submit it late without penalty, if that's possible. It won't be possible if you don't inform your instructor ahead of time that you won't be in class.

If you are sick and won't be able to get to school to turn in work, get someone else to drop off the work in the instructor's office or at the classroom at the beginning of class. If that's impossible, at least call or e-mail the instructor explaining the situation. Your instructor may give you a break if you make that kind of effort and show genuine concern.

How to Behave in Class

Come to class ready to do the work of a professional student. College teachers have no patience for junior high antics and rude behavior in the classroom. Below are some of the behaviors that teachers intensely dislike:

—Carrying on a whispered conversation with a neighbor while the teacher or another student is addressing the class. These conversations are always audible and disturbing. Some students seem to be addicted to jabbering in this manner. This particular behavior can get you kicked out of class

—Expressing a surly or bored attitude, verbally or through body language; being uncooperative

—Sleeping in class

—Eating in class

—Doing homework for another course in class

—Doing homework for this course that was due at the beginning of the period

—Taking beeper messages or cellular phone calls during class; turn these instruments off before entering the classroom

—Drifting into the classroom five minutes late, after the instructor has just finished running through important class business or outlining the work for the day

—Sneaking out early or just getting up and walking out of class before the period ends, without any explanation

Sometimes you can't help being a few minutes late for class. If that happens once, and you go up to the instructor after class and apologize, then no harm done. Sometimes you have to leave early. Get permission from your instructor at the beginning of the class. If your reason is legitimate, most teachers don't mind excusing you early.

If you are taking a class that meets just before your composition course, and the instructor in that earlier class keeps students late, talk to your composition instructor about it. Your composition instructor might have a talk with your other teacher, getting permission for you to leave that class on time. In any case, your composition teacher will know that your lateness is not your fault.

Show interest in what's going on in the course. Raise your hand and answer questions or volunteer to put something on the blackboard. Ask questions in class. You don't have to be an apple polisher, but don't sit in the back of the room like a mushroom growing on the furniture, never speaking, never participating.

It doesn't do any harm to dress neatly. In college, you are entering an adult world, and what was cool in high school often appears silly at this next, professional level of education. If you're at a four-year school, take a look at how the juniors and seniors dress. If you're at a two-year school, model yourself after the older students.

And guys—take your baseball caps off in class. When you are wearing a hat, the teacher can't see your whole head, and if the bill is forward, your face is in shadow. Your composition instructor almost certainly wants to know you personally and be able to recognize you inside and outside the classroom. Teachers see their classrooms as their own personal domain for the duration of the class. Wearing a hat indoors in that domain is disrespectful to the teacher. It's not what works.

2-4 Understand Your Assignments

Composition assignments can be complex. Your instructor may want you to produce a particular kind of essay which exhibits certain features learned in class or from your textbooks. There may be length, line spacing, and other formatting requirements. Don't be staring out the window when your instructor is talking about the next assignment.

Box 2-2 presents a list of information you should acquire about any major writing assignment in composition. Don't be afraid to raise your hand in class and ask for clarification of any of the issues listed in Box 2.2. If you are seriously confused about the assignment, see your instructor after class. Before starting a paper, make sure you know what is expected of you.

Box 2-2 Important Information about Assignments

Make sure you know:

1. Due dates for rough drafts and the final version
2. The length and format requirements (for example, 800-1,000 words, double-spaced text)
3. The type of essay (for example, a "personal narrative" or an "argument on a controversial issue"); a standard designation of essay type, if your instructor offers one, will be useful when you go to the writing center and it will help you turn to the appropriate section in this book for help
4. The learning goals, including any specific in-class learning that is supposed to be evident in the essay (such as proper form for quotations or proper use of the apostrophe)
5. Any organizational requirement (for example, a formal introduction and conclusion; or a point-by-point comparison)
6. Any content requirement (for example, information from an online source; or at least one quotation)
7. Any specified audience, or imagined reader, other than the instructor
8. The criteria for grading; your instructor may have created an evaluation scale showing the relative weight given to sentence correctness, appropriate style, content development, and other features
9. Whether a model essay is available, and if so, how that essay fulfills the assignment.

2-5 Overcome Writer's Block

The worst way to write a composition is to wait until the last minute before it is due and then dash off something to turn in. Yet many students operate that way because they suffer from writer's block, the inability to produce text. In the case of college students, the "block" is usually due to feelings of dread and dislike: "Oh, no, do I *really* have to write a composition? I *hate* writing compositions!" So they put it off and put it off.

Here's how to get around that problem. Write down a schedule or timetable for the whole writing project. Your timetable should begin with very easy tasks for the first one or two sessions, so that you won't neglect them because you hate doing the work. For example, if you have to invent your own topic for this assignment, make inventing the topic your first duty. You're going to sit down and do that before dinner tonight. When you've done that, you're through for the day. Though, if you feel you have the strength, you might also jot down a title and even one or two ideas that you will develop. On the second session, you will write one paragraph on one idea.

Now you're rolling. Once you get started with a paper, you will find it much easier to keep on writing. Your goal should be to get the first draft done early enough to review it and improve it before turning it in. Be sure to *write down* a timetable that will get you to that goal in time. Remember, make the first tasks very easy. If you're not afraid to get started, you will soon find yourself working ahead of your own schedule.

By the way, this is a good approach to any repugnant duty, not just writing compositions. Got a basement you need to clean out? An Incomplete grade you need to make up from last semester? Create a timetable, and make the first tasks easy.

Dread is not the only cause of writer's block for college students. Some students have trouble thinking up topics to write on. Section 7-2 in Chapter 7 provides solutions to this problem, but, in short, you should draw your topics from the things you know about through your home life, school, work, hobbies, sports, and unusual experiences. You can also write about things you are interested in but don't yet know about, in which case you will have to begin by doing some research. The best writers are passionate about their subjects, and they take the trouble to become experts. Don't hesitate to research even those topics you already know a lot about. Take the attitude that all papers are research papers, even the short, single-paragraph essay.

2-6 Get Your Writing Critiqued

Professional writers are always looking for people to read and comment on their pieces of writing. They hound their spouses and friends, and rely on their editors for feedback. They know that the more critiquing they get, and the more they revise on the basis of those critiques, the better their final version will be. So the general rule is: Get as many critiques as you can.

To that end, your instructor may organize your class so that you are working throughout the term with a writing partner or a writing group. Writing partners and groups read your drafts and make comments. You might think that this is the blind leading the blind, but it isn't. Although your instructor can perform a better critique than your fellow students, the students can tell you if they find a sentence or paragraph confusing or if they would like to hear more about a certain idea. In other words, they can give very useful revision guidance, so that the version you submit later to the instructor for a critique is in an advanced form, rather than an early rough form. That, in turn, will make the instructor's suggestions more pertinent to the final version, which will be graded.

If your instructor doesn't assign writing partners or form writing groups, get your own partner or form your own group of three or four students to meet once a week outside of class. On every campus, good students are working in pairs or groups outside of class in many courses, from the freshman year all the way through graduate school. New young professors often form writing groups to help each other get their first scholarly articles published. Those people are doing what works.

In composition, your writing partner or group can provide this kind of critique:

First Impression Check List:

1) ___ fulfills the assignment   ___ isn't doing what the instructor wanted
2) ___ seems complete   ___ needs to be developed more
3) ___ reads smoothly   ___ has some rough spots

Point To's:

1. Point to awkward spots that need rephrasing
2. Point to places where the meaning is unclear
3. Point to places that could be developed more
4. Point to sections that don't seem to belong in the essay or that seem to be out of place
5. Point to any word errors or sentence errors that are noticeable.

For another critique, you can also get your work reviewed at your college's writing center. See the next section for a full discussion of writing centers.

2-7 Use the Writing Center

Writing centers are tutoring facilities for students who are having trouble with a writing assignment or who simply want to improve their writing. Students in pre-composition courses can also get help with grammar and sentence work.

These facilities are not just for weak students. In fact, it is often the strong writers, who could get by on their own, who seek out assistance at the campus writing center, while the weak writers, who need help, don't bother to get it.

The tutors are usually graduate and undergraduate English majors. An English faculty member, possibly with a background in composition research, runs the facility and trains the tutors.

Regardless of what kind of composition course you are taking, the writing center is a good place to get your work reviewed before a major revision. In fact, tutors will help you at any stage in your writing, from thinking up a topic to proofreading the final draft. Bring to the writing center everything you have written so far on the assignment, as well as all teacher handouts and your own notes pertaining to the nature of the assignment.

However, don't bring a half-finished first draft into the center and say, "Help me! The final version is due in one hour!" Writing tutors cannot turn back the clock.

In a well-run writing center with trained staff, the tutors will assist you without writing your paper for you. You should do almost as much talking as the tutor, as the two of you examine your work. Retain ownership of your paper. Don't let the tutor take over or write in any changes. You are the only one who should physically make changes to your text. You are not obliged to follow the tutor's advice. Follow only the suggestions that make sense to you.

Some students feel confident about their ability to compose an essay, but worry about errors in grammar, capitalization, word choice, and so forth. In the opinion of most instructors, getting editing help at the writing center is not cheating—it's learning—and you shouldn't feel guilty about it. In fact, you may learn more about correctness in the writing center than in the classroom, because you will be looking at the specific problems that you have, in the context of your own kinds of sentences, instead of looking abstractly at the huge gamut of problems that arise among all composition students.

2-8 Plan Your Essays

Educators who do research in composition have found that when students plan their essays, they write better papers and get higher grades.

Planning is writing, not busy work.

Except perhaps for the long research paper, your planning does not have to be formal. Just taking the time to think up main topic headings or main ideas, and putting them in a list, helps you see where you are going with the whole paper as you begin to write. With that overview in mind, you won't waste time pursuing lines of thinking that you'll later eliminate as irrelevant. Some effective writers, after creating a general plan, start working on the easiest part. That overcomes writer's block, gets them going.

Don't adhere to your initial plan inflexibly. Change it as you go along, if a new and better content or organization occurs to you.

2-9 Revise Your Essays

Revision, like planning, leads to better texts, better grades.

For student writers, revision too often means small fixes on the word or sentence level. For experienced writers, revision means re-seeing (re-visioning) the text and making major changes to create a new version.

Revise with a big roller, not a small brush.

Be your own toughest critic. About each section, ask yourself questions like these: "Am I being clear? Will this convince my reader? Do I need to say more? Do I sound educated and reasonable?"

And use outside critiques as a basis for revision. That's the whole purpose of getting critiques—to set up revision.

Pulitzer Prize winning author Donald Murray once wrote that great writing "is the distillate of enormous failure." Professional writers take chances, discard their failures, and develop their successes. They look at their favorite passage, realize that it isn't serving the purpose of the text, and cut it. They read their first draft, put it in the bottom of the birdcage where it belongs, and start a new one. No self-pity, no quitting. Just back to work.

Developing a sophisticated writing process includes developing that tough-mindedness about your own texts.

If this makes writing seem like a lot of hard labor, that's because it is. Even for professionals. In fact, one of the biggest differences between professional writers and beginning writers is that the professionals know how much work it takes to produce a good text. They write so much better than beginners partly because they plan and research more, they do more revising, they spend more time fussing with sentences.

2-10 Edit Your Final Drafts

Many composition instructors value good content higher than error-free sentences, but even they inevitably become irritated as they encounter more and more word and sentence errors while reading a paper. If your essay is filled with errors and awkward expressions, your instructor will be in a bad frame of mind by the time he or she is ready to make a grade decision. Obviously, that doesn't bode well for you.

The purpose of editing is the improvement of word choices, individual sentences, and short sequences of sentences. When editing your paper, you look for places where the words and phrasing are:

- unclear
- ugly
- wrong in their effect on the readers (perhaps scaring them about the difficulty of a process when you should be reassuring them that they will be able to do it)
- wrong in tone (perhaps too informal for an academic essay; or too stuffy)
- too wordy (you're taking twenty words to say something that can be said in six; or you're just repeating yourself)
- inconsistent with standard word usage (for example, using a local dialect meaning of a word that wouldn't

be understood by people outside the area, such as *ignorant* to mean "ill mannered")

- ungrammatical.

Editing is one chore your writing partner or writing group members can help you with. In fact, you can have a session in which you do nothing but edit each other's compositions, looking for the problems listed above. The writing center tutor will also help you with editing, once your composition has been adequately developed.

Editing for clarity is an extremely important activity and one that you should focus on strongly. Often when a clarity problem is fixed, other problems in the list above disappear at the same time. When editing for clarity, you have to imagine yourself as a stranger, a person who can't read your mind and therefore depends entirely on what you have put down on paper. So make sure that your sentences fully deliver your meaning. The reader, not having access to your outline and other planning materials, moves through your essay somewhat in the dark, not knowing what's coming up next. You can help out there by creating sign post sentences that guide the reader through the essay:

> Besides better speed, the catamaran sailboat also has the advantage of more stability.

That sentence tells the reader that you are through discussing "speed" and will now discuss "stability."

Grammaticality is the most difficult editing problem. If you don't know that something is ungrammatical, you normally won't notice the problem. Yet, sometimes, your unconscious language knowledge can help you sense that something is wrong. Try reading your paper aloud, listening for phrasing that doesn't sound quite right. When you find such a spot, try revising the phrasing until it sounds better.

Few college students at any level know all the rules of formal written grammar and correct word use. In fact, as students move through college, their error rates often go up for a period of time, as the complexity of their sentences and vocabulary increases and, consequently, the opportunity for error increases. For example, subject-verb agreement errors (such as a singular subject and a plural verb) occur most often when intervening words separate the subject and verb. College juniors and seniors tend to embed more words between subjects and verbs than freshmen do, resulting in more subject-verb agreement errors.

Ungrammaticality is not a problem you are going to completely solve in a first year composition course. Learning correct Standard English comes about slowly over time, partly unconsciously through reading and listening to educated speech, and partly through conscious effort. The inevitable slowness of learning in this area, however, does not exempt you from trying your best to turn in essays devoid of grammatical error or improper word usage. Getting critiques—having others read and comment on your writing—is one way to work on this problem. As the next section shows, using an English handbook and usage dictionary is another.

2-11 Use Reference Books

English handbooks point out certain kinds of common errors and list rules for capitalization, punctuation, use of italics, and so forth. Your instructor will probably assign a handbook for your course, but if not, buy one on your own. You'll find it useful throughout college. Diana Hacker's *A Pocket Style Manual* is a good example of this kind of guide. It's short and clearly written, and therefore appropriate for beginning writers. For a more dense version of a handbook, in a package not much bigger than a deck of cards, you might get *Langenscheidt's Pocket Merriam-Webster Guide to Punctuation and Style.*

Once you own a handbook, explore it, find out what's in there, and then use it. Don't toss it in a corner and leave it to gather dust. If you need to know what words to capitalize in a title or whether to write "who" or "whom," don't guess, look it up in the handbook. You may not be successful in finding an answer every time, but you'll get better at that with practice.

A specialized dictionary of English usage can help you determine exactly what a word means and how it can be properly used. A student once wrote: "I raced up the stairs, and when I got to the top I was feeling very effete." Perhaps his thesaurus had told him that *effete* meant "worn out." But *Webster's Dictionary of English Usage* tells us that the word *effete* is "not suggestive of exhaustion so much as of refinement, weakness of character, snobbery, and effeminacy." Unlike regular dictionaries, usage dictionaries focus on problem words and provide detailed explanations of how those words should, and should not, be used.

If you want to get serious about using words correctly, buy a usage dictionary to accompany your regular dictionary. Besides *Webster's* mentioned above, *The American Heritage Book of English Usage* is a good resource, as is Bryan Garner's *A Dictionary of Modern American Usage.* You might also consider S.I. Hayakawa and Eugene Ehrlich's *Choose the Right Word*, which shows the different connotations of similar words, such as *eradicate* and *expunge.* Use **www.bestbookbuys.com** to get the best online prices.

Don't let the complexity of word usage scare you away from trying out new words, even if it means occasionally making a mistake. Language learning is always accompanied by error. After all, to learn you have to step beyond what you already know into a realm of uncertainty. Plunge into the English language. It's your language, by birthright or by adoption. You own it—start taking possession of it.

2-12 Proofread Your Final Drafts

After you have edited your text and you are satisfied with its content and phrasing, it is time to proofread. Proofreading means reading over your text looking for typographical errors. These are recognizable accidents that your computer's spell checker won't pick up, such as "I sheep" when you meant "I sleep," and missing words, such as *to* in "I went school." Instructors may forgive grammatical errors to some extent, but they have little patience for typographical errors that have been left uncorrected.

A student at a state university handed in a paper with sentences like these: I really think any coach give a player a hard time. Here's what he had intended: I really **don't** think any coach **should** give a player a hard time.

Imagine the difficulty of reading and interpreting such a paper. Imagine the mood of the composition instructor when deciding what grade to put on it.

If possible, first get someone else to proofread your paper, such as your writing partner, your roommate, a friend, a writing center tutor. Then proofread it yourself. You must, at some point, do your own proofread, because only you can recognize certain mistakes, such as a wrong number ("the six of us" when it should be "the five of us"). Also, your other proofreader may miss some errors that you will pick up. If you get your final draft back with point deductions for uncorrected typos, you can go to your instructor and moan that a writing center tutor proofread it or your writing partner proofread it, but don't expect any sympathy. You must do the final check, and you are responsible for any errors that remain.

Box 2-3 shows some of the common errors that professional proofreaders look for. The examples are based on real student sentences. Check for those errors in your own text.

Professional proofreaders are effective partly because they know what to look for (such as the items in Box 2-3) and where to look. Errors occur to an uncanny degree in

- titles
- section headings
- the first lines of paragraphs

Box 2-3 Common Proofreading Errors

Missing words

TEXT: I really think any coach give a player a hard time.

INTENDED: I really **don't** think any coach **should** give a player a hard time.

Missing word parts

TEXT: When that employee see that both customer have. . . .

INTENDED: When that employee see**s** that both customer**s** have. . . .

Word part substitutions

TEXT: He shouldn't be knocked it.

INTENDED: He shouldn't be knock**ing** it.

A missing period, end parenthesis, or end quotation mark

Missing end quote:

TEXT: According to Anderson, "School grammar is hard to learn partly because English grammar is not nearly as simple or consistent as it is made out to be in textbooks. For example, pronouns, in reality, don't always refer to something in the text.

INTENDED: According to Anderson, "School grammar is hard to learn partly because English grammar is not nearly as simple or consistent as it is made out to be in textbooks." For example, pronouns, in reality, don't always refer to something in the text.

Transposed letters

TEXT: teh   INTENDED: the

Transposed words

TEXT: how well I can the do work

INTENDED: how well I can do the work

Alternate correct spellings

Sometimes writing *online* and other times writing *on-line*/ alternately writing *theatre* and *theater*

List format errors

Creating a vertical list in which the elements don't line up; misnumbering items in a numbered list

Obvious capitalization errors

Such as failing to capitalize a person's name: Jeff mcQuillan wrote. . . .

Widows and orphans

A last page consisting of only a single line; a section title at the bottom of a page

Reference errors

Referring to Figure 2 as Figure 3; referring the reader to page 2 for a passage that actually appears on page 1; failing to provide a bibliographic entry for a parenthetical note in the text

Bad math

Mistakes in arithmetic; breaking something down into percentages that don't add up to 100

- the first element in a vertical list
- anywhere that the typeface suddenly changes, such as a change in font size or a shift from plain text to italics.

Do a first proofread of those places, before reviewing the whole text.

Unlike grammatical errors, proofreading errors are always recognizable as errors, if noticed. Your job is to spot them. Professionals use methods that you can adopt. They're designed to force you to focus on the words on the page, instead of reading simply for meaning. Have you noticed that after reading a few pages of a book, you have a sense of the meaning of what you just read, but you can't remember seeing any of the sentences? To avoid that "text blindness," try one or more of the three approaches to proofreading listed below, especially if you are having trouble spotting your mistakes. Try the first one, and if that doesn't work for you, try the second, and if you are still missing errors, go to the third method.

1. Read your essay aloud, slowly, carefully pronouncing each word.
2. Read your text backwards a line at a time, from the last line to the first.
3. Cut a one inch by four inch rectangle from a piece of cardboard or a manila folder; then cut a small rectangular window in that, so that you can read about four words looking through the window. Place your cardboard piece on the text and read slowly through the window.

2-13 Eliminate the Five Bugaboos

When you are editing and proofreading, make sure that you eliminate certain common errors that drive composition instructors up the wall. Students have been making these same trivial mistakes for centuries, and for centuries these nasty little mishaps have aroused feelings of anguish and despair in the souls of English teachers.

Look for these problems:

1) **Confusing *its* with *it's*.** The first means "belongs to *it*," as in The dog ate its bone; the second means "it is," as in It's going to rain today. Memory trick: Think of the apostrophe in *it's* as standing for the dot in the *i* in *is*.

2) **Confusing *to* with *too*.** Use the first with verbs: He likes to swim. And use it to point in a direction: He went to the park. Use *too* to mean more than desired: He drives too fast / That steak is too well done. Memory trick: The word *too* has too many *o*'s in it.

    Use *too* also to mean "also": She, too, likes to swim / He likes to help, too. Memory trick: *too* has an *o* and "also" another *o*.

3) **Confusing *there*, *their*, and *they're*.** The first is a pointing word: Your book is over there. It also functions as a meaningless filler in *there is* / *there are* constructions: There is nothing funny about that. The second means "belonging to them": That is their book. The third means "they are": They're ready to go.

4) **Confusing *of* with *have*.** When *have* is an auxiliary verb (He should have helped his mother) it is sometimes pronounced the same way *of* is pronounced, but it is never spelled that way. This is **wrong**: He should of helped his mother.

5) **Confusing *where* with *were*.** Don't forget the silent *h* in *where*: Where were you? This is **wrong**: He came to were I lived.

If necessary, conduct a final editing session in which you do nothing but make computer searches for these troublesome words to make sure that you have spelled them correctly. Or if working with a hard copy, read over the text once just for these words and mark them with a highlighter. Then, referring to the above discussion as necessary, evaluate each marked word for correctness.

2-14 Turn In Neat Copy

Assuming you are turning in word processed texts to your instructor, the essays you submit will probably have a clean appearance. Probably. Alas, some students manage to make text from a laser printer look awful: no margin on one side, odd font changes, strange indentations or no paragraphing at all.

A sloppy appearance gives a bad impression of you and your work. It's immature and rude.

Grading is always somewhat subjective. You want your teacher in a good mood when it comes time to make the grading decision. Composition instructors have to wade through stacks of papers, so they value neatness. It's easier on the eyes and brain. It makes their work less frustrating. Even if you are a casual kind of person who doesn't mind an errant sock lying on the bedroom floor, make the papers you submit to others as neat as possible. It's part of doing what works.

2-15 Take Advantage of Instructor Conferences

Many programs require you to meet once or twice during the term with your instructor for an extended conference. In this conference, you and your instructor discuss your progress in the course, as well as your immediate writing project.

Even if such conferences are not a part of your course, you can schedule a meeting with your instructor at any time during the term. You should do so if you are having trouble with the course. Your instructor may be able to get you on the right track. For example, if you are getting low grades on your essays, the marginal written comments on those papers may not fully explain what you need to do to improve. However, your instructor may be able to make that clear during a conference.

You are much better off arranging such a meeting in the first third of the term than in the last third, when it may be too late to salvage your grade. In other words, don't put it off. Start looking for solutions at the first sign of trouble.

2-16 Become a Reader

Becoming an educated person is a long journey, and becoming an habitual reader is one of the smartest first steps you can take. Knowledge resides mainly in the written word.

There are other benefits to reading besides acquiring information. If you're a native speaker of English, you learned the grammar and rhetoric of spoken English as an infant through oral contact with the language. Children deprived of contact with other speakers during this critical age never develop fluency in language. Likewise, you cannot learn the grammar and rhetoric of written English without contact with written texts. The more contact, the better.

Leave magazines, newspapers, and books around your home, so that everywhere you alight, there's something to read. Read in bed before falling off to sleep. Read in the bathroom. Read while the TV commercials are playing.

You don't have to start with a ponderous volume of antique verse or a dense philosophical treatise. Start with subjects that interest you: sports, hobbies, love stories, horror stories—it doesn't matter. Gradually introduce other kinds of texts, experimentally, to deepen your intake of information and to broaden your contact with different styles of writing. Your unconscious mind will do most of the work, but it doesn't hurt to occasionally notice how a writer is saying things. This is painless learning.

2-17 Stay Healthy

Have you heard of the "freshman fifteen"? That's the extra weight first year students sometimes gain from gorging on grease burgers and mindlessly munching snacks. The stress of starting college and the absence of healthy home cooked meals can lead to poor eating habits and other behaviors damaging to your health and your performance as a student. It is no accident that students come down with mononucleosis, the flu, and other debilitating diseases so frequently. Those germs attack stressed out bodies weakened from lack of sleep, too much partying, and bad diets.

It's tough to pass composition, or any other college course, if a serious illness knocks you out of class for three weeks. In fact, your grades can suffer if you miss just a few days of classes at a crucial time when important work is coming due.

As much as possible, stay away from the grease and sugar, and eat some hearty soups and salads. If you must drink alcohol, use your college years to develop sophisticated tastes. Learn to sip and savor expensive, high quality beers and wines, instead of guzzling gallons of Yellow Water Pilsner and Rot Gut Red. Become a social drinker, instead of a boorish drunk.

Last but not least, exercise. Most colleges provide equipment that you can check out for free or rent cheaply: tennis rackets, cross country skis, basketballs, canoes. Many campuses now have health club facilities with exercise machines and swimming pools. Exercise programs are available for the handicapped. Regular workouts are good not only for keeping in shape but also for relieving stress. While you're jogging or pumping iron or swimming laps, you can be composing the first draft of your composition in your head, or figuring out how you're going to revise the latest draft.

Exercise refreshes the body and spirit and gives you energy to do the hard work of studying and writing. In the first year of college especially, moving the old body around is one of the smartest moves you can make.

2-18 Avoid Obsessive Behaviors

If you find yourself doing one thing to excess, you're in trouble. Some students get caught up in games, like pool or bridge or Dungeons & Dragons, and waste away the day playing instead of working. Others party every night. Some fall so much in love with one course that they obsessively study that subject and ignore their other classes.

Philosophers throughout the ages have advised humanity about the need for balance in life and the value of moderation. Get wise. If you find yourself substituting a diversion for responsible work, or becoming intensely attracted to one intellectual activity, step back and think about what you are doing.

2-19 Check on Your Grade If You Think It May Be Wrong

The term is over. You get your report card and—yikes! You thought you were going to get at least a C in composition, and maybe a B, but instead the card says D!

In that case, check with your instructor to make sure there wasn't a clerical error. The instructor can make a mistake when entering your grade on a grade sheet, and the clerk who transfers that grade from the sheet to the computer can make a typing error.

If there was no clerical error and you strongly believe you deserve a higher grade, you have the option of following the formal grade appeal process at your school. Don't hang around the instructor's office whining and pleading. The college catalogue will describe the appropriate process. You will have to present a reasoned argument and documentation, such as your essays. Some English departments will appoint a neutral professor to read your work and evaluate it. A warning, though. Administrators and colleagues are going to be reluctant to overturn a professor's grading decision, unless there is strong reason to do so. And that's the way it should be. So don't waste your own time or the college's by challenging grades just to see if you can luck out. The appeal process is for times when you are certain you deserve a higher grade, and you feel confident that you can demonstrate that.

If your appeal doesn't work out, take solace in the fact that nearly every student at some point in college gets a grade lower than expected, or even deserved. It's not a pleasant experience, but it's not the end of the world, either. Keep things in perspective, move on.

Part II

Meeting the Challenges of Academic Writing

Academic writing has its own set of tasks and requirements, and composition students struggle with several of them. This section looks at three of the most difficult and most important challenges of academic writing: full development of points, educated adult reasoning, and incorporation of outside sources.

3

Developing Your Points

Professional writers often write too much and have to cut back, but beginners have the opposite problem—they don't write enough to effectively achieve their purposes, such as persuading or usefully informing or providing an interesting interpretation.

The cycle of critique and revision will be more useful to you if you bring to it a fully developed first draft. This chapter shows you how to do that.

3-1 Approach the Blank Screen with a Busy Mind

An experienced writer rarely, if ever, begins writing an essay cold. Instead, the writer's mind is warmed up and swirling with ideas, even if they are somewhat vague. Below are three "pre-writing" activities that you can engage in, so that you start writing with something to say.

Day Dream

After your instructor has assigned a composition, don't "put it out of your mind" as you leave the classroom. Start thinking about it while you walk across the campus. And keep on thinking about it whenever possible: while walking, eating, driving, lazing around, waiting in line, jogging, doing yard work, etc. Start writing parts of the essay in your head. Talk to your readers and listen to them respond to you; imagine them questioning your meaning or disagreeing with what you are saying.

Talk Aloud

Sometimes instructors will ask students to explain orally to the class what they plan to say in their next paper. This forces the students to bring together vague thoughts in their minds and begin to articulate them and form them into a coherent whole. You can do this on your own. Find someone to talk to about your paper. Say to a friend, "Hey, I've got to write a paper that teaches people about something I'm an expert on. What do you think of this idea. I'll talk about the benefits of hiking and describe some of the great hiking spots in this area." And keep on talking.

If your friend won't listen, or you're embarrassed to talk about your work to another person, then wait until you are alone and talk aloud to an imaginary version of your friend, or some other audience. Explain your purpose in writing, what you hope to accomplish, and how you are going to achieve that purpose. You'll be making all this up as you go along, of course, but that's the whole idea.

Doodle and Scribble

You can also think on paper. A lot of early idea-generation activity is best done at super speed. In *free writing*, you simply start writing quickly about your subject, putting down anything, however silly, that comes to mind. If you stall, you start repeating—rewriting—the last few words you wrote over and over until new ones come to you. *Listing* is a similar approach. Quick—list three thoughts about your subject. When you've done that, look at the first thought you've written down and quickly list three thoughts about it.

Mapping is for those who like visual planning. Start with an oval shaped bubble in the middle of a page and then write in that bubble your central purpose: *Encourage more students to vote*. Then draw a couple of lines out from the central bubble and draw balloons or bubbles attached to them. In this case, you might put *why* in one and a *how* in the other. Additional balloons off the "why" bubble would indicate the reasons you will present.

Listing and mapping, besides generating ideas, also suggest an organization to your essay, what the main parts will be and how specific points will be grouped.

3-2 Teach Your Subject

A well-known writing expert, Linda Flower, advises students to "teach" their subject. This is a useful conceptualization of what a good writer does. Note the difference between these two passages:

> Another reason for opposing doctor-assisted suicide is that it violates the Hippocratic Oath. That oath tells doctors to never give up on life.

> Another reason for opposing doctor-assisted suicide is that it violates the Hippocratic Oath. That oath, written in the 5th century B.C. by the influential Greek doctor Hippocrates, says in part: "I will not give a drug that is deadly to anyone if asked, nor will I suggest the way to such a counsel." The Hippocratic Oath has been a standard for medical ethics for some 2,400 years. It should not be tossed aside lightly.

Do you see the "teaching" in that second passage? Because of that teaching, the argument the writer makes is clearer, more interesting, more memorable, and more convincing. Of course, to teach your subject you have to know about it. You might be thinking right now: "But I don't know those details about the Hippocratic Oath." Well then, use an Internet search engine like Altavista or Google to search the Web for the Hippocratic Oath. Or look up the oath in an encyclopedia. Get in the habit of pausing to do a bit of quick learning as you write.

In the same vein, learn the vocabulary of your subject. Here's another example of thin and thick development:

The young woman I fell instantly in love with that summer was thin and had a mass of blond curls. I first saw her at the boat rental dock.

The young woman I fell instantly in love with that cool summer morning had spindling arms and legs, like a kid. Yet her face was expansive: a wide smile, blue eyes far apart, a chaotic mass of blonde curls extending her visage all around. She was looking right at me when I first saw her. We stared at each other for a moment, and then she blushed and turned away, her pallid cheek now crimson. She was standing on the boat rental dock and I immediately fantasized about getting into a rowboat with her and drifting off into the morning mist.

Again, the writer's purpose is advanced by the fuller development. The effect of the young woman, at first sight, on the writer comes through more clearly. You sense the strength of his burgeoning romantic feelings.

You may be thinking, "But I don't know words like *spindling, expansive, visage,* and *pallid.*" Use your dictionary and thesaurus to explore the vocabulary of your subject. If you are concerned with physical description of a person, take some time to find, and examine the exact meanings of, words pertaining to the kind of face and physique you want to describe. It's easier to bring in details when you have the words for them.

When you know the language and the facts of your subject, you can take your subject, even if it's romantic love, and teach it.

3-2 Mark Words and Sentences for Expansion

If you're having trouble thinking up things to say about your subject that will advance your purposes, try this method. From your first draft, underline important words, phrases, or sentences. Then turn them into lead-off generalizations—topic sentences—for whole new paragraphs or even pages. In the paragraph below, the writer has underlined some words that can be developed usefully:

> Indexing is so <u>important</u> that high-tech companies often out-source the job to professional freelance indexers. However, indexing is <u>expensive</u>, so some companies try to save money by <u>training</u> one of their own staff to do the indexing.

The subject is the indexing of technical manuals, and the author wants to inform the reader that indexing is very important, but unfortunately expensive. The first two underlined words directly address those main points: it's <u>important</u> and it's <u>expensive</u>. The last, <u>training</u>, is a solution to a problem. Solutions are usually worth discussing in detail. Here are the main points (in bold) and an expansion of each one:

> **Indexing is very important for manuals that document high-tech products.** Customers don't want to read three or four hundred pages to learn a particular fact or to remind themselves how to carry out some small operation. The table of contents can be helpful for finding major topics in a dense manual, but for zeroing in on a very specific topic, only an index will do.
>
> **Unfortunately, indexing is expensive.** A professional indexer might charge $800 to $1000 to index a short, 200-page manual. Longer manuals will obviously cost more. Although this investment is almost always worth it, some companies operating on a tight budget can't afford it.
>
> **One way that companies get around the heavy expense is to train one of their own employees.** It might cost $400 in tuition fees and another $300 in travel expenses to send a technical writer to a two-day indexing workshop, but that's cheap when you consider how quickly the company will recoup that investment by not having to outsource indexing. Of course, the company is still paying for indexing, in the sense that it pays the technical writer a wage, but the technical writer is a salaried employee. Consultants and service contractors charge huge hourly sums, often triple the hourly rate of a salaried employee.

In the expanded version, the importance of indexing is first made clearer by the explanation as to *why* it is important. The expense has now been stated in enough detail so that the reader knows what the writer means by "expensive" (not $100 and not $10,000, but around $1,000 for a 200-page text). And finally, because of the expansion, the reader better understands the cost-effectiveness of doing indexing in-house. All in all, by better informing the reader about the subject, the writer gets the main points across more clearly and convincingly.

In your own essays, try the following approaches to expanding words, phrases, or sentences into whole paragraphs or whole pages:

a) **Provide descriptive detail.** Instead of "The room was a <u>mess</u>, so I wearily started to clean it," write that the room was a mess and then describe the mess: unmade bed, clothes on the floor, ash tray with ashes, waste basket overflowing. You can further describe the <u>unmade bed</u> and the <u>clothes</u> on the floor. Using a thesaurus and dictionary, develop some vocabulary, like *slovenly, disarray, tousled, clutter.* A word like *clutter* you already know, but might not think to use. Exploring the vocabulary of your subject not only introduces you to new words but also brings to mind familiar ones. And rubbing shoulders with vocabulary helps you to generate ideas.

b) **List examples.** Let's start with this paragraph:

> Not all weight control methods are agonizing. Female students here at Pumpkinville College can also play <u>intramural sports</u> as a way of keeping off the 'freshman fifteen,' while having a lot of fun. Even taking a <u>long walk</u> after dinner helps. (41 words)

Now let's develop "intramural sports" and "long walk" by providing examples:

Not all weight control methods are agonizing. Female students here at Pumpkinville College can also play intramural sports as a way of keeping off the 'freshman fifteen,' while having a lot of fun. In the fall, women can play on one of the soccer teams. In the winter, they can join the basketball league. In spring, there's the softball league.

Even taking a long walk after dinner helps. Those who live in one of the dorms can take a stroll downtown and back. Those who live in an apartment in town can take a nice walk along the river bank. (98 words)

Going from 41 words to 98 words by providing examples doesn't just lengthen your paper, it adds useful information. If your purpose as a writer at this point is to encourage students to exercise, you have advanced that purpose by giving readers examples of exercise available to them.

c) **Develop a single example.** Sometimes you can expand your text with a single, elaborate example that demonstrates your point:

Not all weight control methods are agonizing. As a female student here at Pumpkinville College, you can also play intramural sports as a way of keeping off the 'freshman fifteen,' while enjoying yourself at the same time. In the fall, for example, you can play on one of the intramural soccer teams. While playing soccer, you run up and down a huge field for a couple of hours. Just as important, you are frequently twisting, changing direction, sprinting and slowing down, kicking, falling down and getting up. It's like a planned exercise program, but instead of quitting after 20 minutes, you keep doing it for an hour or two because it's fun.

d) **Provide evidence.** Evidence makes your assertions more believable, while at the same time expanding your text with impressive development. Let's say that you've written this statement: "Despite what you hear from politicians and newspaper columnists, American public schools are doing a great job. Therefore, ..." *Hey, wait a minute!* your reader might be thinking, *before you get into your "therefore . . . ," convince me*:

> Despite what you hear from politicians or newspaper columnists, American public schools are doing a great job. Young people who went to public schools in the 1980s and 1990s were well educated and better educated than any group in the history of the country. The non-partisan Center on Education Policy provides important statistics about public school performance at **www.aypf.org**. They note that in the past two decades, more students than ever before took difficult advanced courses; that NAEP scores have gone up for all grade levels, especially in math and science; that math and verbal SAT scores rose during the 1990s, even though more students from traditionally low-scoring groups began taking the test; that ACT scores have risen steadily since 1983, even though "record numbers of students are taking the exam—a factor that normally would cause scores to drop."

e) **Explain how.** You have written this statement: "You should make your instructions easy to understand." Ok, now develop your text by telling your readers *how.*

> You should make your instructions easy to understand. Avoid technical terms, or at least define them. Use illustrations. Number the steps.

Each one of those developing statements names a process that could also be expanded with more *how's.* How do you define terms? How do you use illustrations effectively? How do different numbering formats work?

f) Explain why. You start with this:

> The one-handed backhand in tennis is better than the two-handed backhand. So, as assistant coach of the high school team, I began to encourage the younger players to switch to the one-hander.

Let's revise with more development, telling *why.*

> The one-handed backhand in tennis is better than the two-handed backhand. With the one-hander, you can easily hit top spin or slice, but with the two-hander you can only hit top spin with ease. The one-hander allows you to stretch further and reach balls you can't get to with the two-hander. So, as assistant coach of the high school team, I began to encourage the younger players to switch to the one-hander.

g) Make comparisons. A comparison shows either similarities or differences between two things. If you want to show young people that a catamaran sailboat would be a good choice for them, instead of just naming the catamaran's features, extend your development by comparing those features with those of a monohull boat. Instead of writing this

> A catamaran is a good boat for teenagers because it's fast and wet, and it can be tilted at a daring angle.

write this

> A catamaran is a better sailboat for young people than a monohull. The catamaran is fast. The monohull, by contrast, is sometimes painfully slow. Even with very little wind, the catamaran will be moving, while the monohull bobs in the water and those aboard bake in the sun. On a catamaran, you can enhance the thrill of a strong wind by

riding on one hull. This tilts the boat at a tremendous angle, while you hang in the wind to keep it from tipping over. In a monohull, a strong wind will tilt the boat somewhat, but that thrill is less than riding five feet above the water on a catamaran hull. Finally, the cat is a wet boat, so you get a lot of spray, while the monohull is a dry boat for those who don't like water in their face.

Of course, you can always extend the development even further. Your first point is that a catamaran is faster than a monohull. So, explain *why*:

A catamaran is a better sailboat for young people than a monohull. First of all, the catamaran is fast, which naturally appeals to youngsters who want some thrills out there on the water. Even with very little wind, the catamaran will be moving, while the monohull bobs in the water and those aboard bake in the sun.

The reason for the speed of the catamaran lies in the hull construction. Any part of the hull that is below water causes drag and slows the boat. The catamaran's two, wide-apart, slim hulls barely touch the water's surface. A 16-ft cat may have a mere fourteen-inch draft with two adults aboard. That means that only fourteen inches of the craft's V-shaped hulls are below water.

The monohull, by contrast, is slow. It needs ballast (weight in the bottom of its hull) for stability. So its wide lead-lined bottom sits low in the water, creating a lot of drag.

In the earlier, less developed version, the writer merely makes a point about speed. In the expanded version, the writer makes the same point more convincingly by teaching the subject.

h) Define terms. You can develop your text by defining terms briefly or extensively. Decisions on whether or not to provide brief definitions are based on reader analysis. You quickly define a term if you think that some of your readers may not be able to figure it out within the context you have provided. Below are two levels of short definition, parenthetical and full sentence. Parenthetical definitions can be punctuated with parentheses or commas:

Using parentheses

The company's style guide avoids diacritical (accent) marks for foreign expressions that have been Anglicized (fully adopted into the English language).

Using commas

When a sailboat jibes, changes direction by turning with its stern to the wind, the boom shifts position with a hard slam.

The full sentence definition is more formal. In this case, instead of defining a term in passing, you halt the progress of your text to define the term with a whole sentence or two.

Using a full sentence

A motor vehicle pursuit is an active attempt by a law enforcement officer, operating a motor vehicle and utilizing siren and emergency lights, to apprehend one or more occupants of another moving vehicle, when the driver of the fleeing vehicle is aware of the attempt and is resisting apprehension by maintaining or increasing speed in excess of the legal speed limit.

—From the *Police Officer Manual*, Pittsburgh, PA

Some composition instructors ask you to develop an extended definition of a complex technical term, such as *Marxism,* or an abstract familiar term such as *friendship.* Box 3-1 shows some standard methods of definition. If you need to define a term, either briefly or extensively, read over the suggestions in Box 3-1 and pick out several approaches that might work for your term and try them out. Your decision as to which methods to employ should be based on which ones most effectively advance your purpose in writing and help your audience understand your text.

Box 3-1 Methods of Definition

Classification and differentiation: A catamaran is a boat with two hulls.

Etymology (word history)**:** The word *computer* comes from the Latin word *computare* meaning "to count."

Negative definition: Phonics is not a method of reading, but of word identification.

Contrast: Terriers are more hyperactive than most other breeds.

Comparison (similarities)**:** Both a cable TV system and a satellite system will provide many channels.

Figurative comparison: Health food is like medicine, only less expensive and without side effects.

Example: Reference books for writers include dictionaries, spelling dictionaries, thesauruses, and word finders.

Purpose: A trip report allows you to share with your supervisors and co-workers what you learned or accomplished on your trip.

Physical description: Terriers tend to have short curly hair.

Operational description (how it works)**:** A vector graphic produces an image through the application of a mathematical formula defining the boundaries of the shape.

Components: A progress report tells the reader how far along you are in the project, what problems you've been having, and what you plan to do next.

3-3 Be Selective

In expanding your paper, don't just add information that is somehow related to the subject being discussed. You can say many things about any given subject—say only what will advance your purpose at the moment and your purpose overall in the essay. If, for example, your purpose is to convince young people that a beach catamaran sailboat would be the best kind of boat for those seeking maximum thrills on the water, don't talk about the history of catamarans or even their beauty. Develop your text with those details that demonstrate the thrilling qualities of the boat. Or, for contrast, show the dullness of other models of sailboat.

3-4 Test Your Essay for Depth

Before deciding that your text is ready for editing, weigh it in your hands, assessing its heft. Is it rather light and thin? If the instructor suggested a paper of 2-4 pages, does yours run only half way down page 2, instead of most of the way down page 4? When you read it over, does it seem to jump quickly from one topic to another? Instead of developing an idea further, are you just repeating yourself?

If so, go back and use the methods discussed here to add some depth.

As a general principle, approach your subject with interest and enthusiasm, becoming educated about it and teaching it to your reader. By adding depth to your content, you make the content more interesting and more effective in achieving your purposes—and that in turn will earn you a higher grade.

4

Sounding Educated

Essays are silent objects, ink on a page, until they are read. Then the author's voice emerges in the reader's mind. The author may sound confident or confused, calm or hysterical, reasonable or biased. You can be certain that your instructor will judge the intelligence of your essays partly on the kind of voice that you project.

How should you try to sound in your compositions? Let's call the appropriate tone for college essays the "educated voice." When you graduate from college, you want your speech and writing to reflect your sophistication. Composition courses are an appropriate place to start adopting an educated voice, and the thought processes that lie behind it. An educated voice is not just big words and fancy phrasing. It reflects a way of thinking about serious subjects, a careful reasoning that intellectual people slowly develop through their education.

Let's begin by making a series of contrasts between an educated and uneducated voice:

Educated	Uneducated
Appropriately Formal	Too Informal
Quiet	Loud
Precise or Understated	Exaggerated
Fair-minded	Pushy
Idea Oriented	Personal
Cautious	Certain

The rest of this chapter examines each of those contrasts.

4-1 Appropriately Formal versus Too Informal

You will have to find out what degree of informality your instructor allows in compositions. This varies from teacher to teacher. However, most composition instructors prefer a fairly formal tone and style similar to that found in scholarly works or newspaper editorials. In such discussions, the writer avoids unnecessary obscenity, slang, and other informal expressions. If you are enrolled in this type of class, you should avoid a too-loose, jazzy style or an informal, conversational style. Here are some examples:

Too jazzy:
Furry Muckers like to jump into the Truth-or-Dare Hot Tub, where they feel each other's tails and stuff. When I first stumbled into FurryMuck (I was a fish named Big Tuna; Wolfoids tried to eat me), I figured it was a very wry college-kid joke thing. It's not. It's quite serious. The place has an apartment complex where 190 people live (if you want housing here, there's a waiting list), many bucolic parks and lakes, a taxi system, and underground caverns. Lots of squirreloids.

> —From a narrative about participation in an online MOO, quoted in *Wired Style: Principles of English Usage in the Digital Age.*

Too conversational:
As for how my high school could be improved, well, I'd start by giving the principle the boot. That jerk ruins everything for everybody. He and my English teacher, Miss Parker. Doesn't she know that not everyone thinks Shakespeare is hot stuff?

Appropriately formal:
If I were on the school board, I would improve the high school I graduated from, first of all, by making certain personnel changes. I would like to hire a new principal who is friendlier to the students than the man we now have in that job. Some of the teachers also present a problem. They don't understand what young people are interested in. English teachers, for example, could have students

read some contemporary stories directly relevant to what is going on in their own lives. If it is worthwhile to also read difficult authors like Shakespeare, we need to hire English teachers who know how to show that to students.

Some instructors value a natural voice, and they lecture against pretentiousness. Essayist Susan Orlean provides a humorous example of the pretentious voice in the first of these two sentences:

> Psychologists identify ten as roughly the age at which many boys experience the gender-linked normative developmental trauma that leaves them, as adult men, at risk for specific psycho-logical sequalae often manifest as deficits in the arenas of intimacy, empathy, and struggles with commitment in relationships. In other words, this is around the age when guys get screwed up about girls.

Orlean was being witty, but some "intellectuals," in all seriousness, write in the style of that first sentence. If you were to do so, you would sound well schooled, but you would also sound pretentious. Your arrogant indifference to your reader, who has to wade through that waist-deep mud, would not pay off in admiration.

Fortunately, the pretentious style is not a problem for most composition students. It is more likely to arise in the writing of graduate students who are trying to sound like the abstruse journals they read.

Start with a formal style and restrained tone, and listen for hints from your instructor as to what levels of formality are permitted. Or raise your hand and ask.

4-2 Quiet versus Loud

Readers associate a quiet tone with reasonableness and education, a loud tone with the opposite. What makes a written tone loud? For the most part, strong words representing strong emotions. Listen to this statement:

> I hate those hypocrites who claim they care about the treatment of animals and then wear leather gloves and fur-lined coats.

Suppose, now, you revised the sentence so that the same thought was expressed quietly:

> Those who care about the treatment of animals should consider not wearing leather gloves and fur-lined coats.

In the second version, you dispensed with strong emotion ("hate") and the name calling ("hypocrites"). You also called off the attack on the sincerity of those who say they care about animals (you removed the word *claim*). Behind this shift in tone is a shift in attitude toward those you disagree with, a recognition that they may be mistaken, but they aren't evil. And a realization that you are going to be more convincing if you speak quietly, than if you shout. Both statements above imply the same thing: that a concern for animals is inconsistent with a willingness to support industries that exploit animals, such as those that deal in leather and fur. A quiet tone allows the reader to focus on the logic behind your words. A loud tone expresses your attitude so strongly that the reader may notice only your vehemence, missing your line of reasoning.

4-3 Precise or Understated versus Exaggerated

The American style of speech accepts exaggeration as normal. We use hyperbole regularly. When we're very hungry, we say we're "starving." When we watch Jerry defeat his racket ball opponent by a significant score we say, "Jerry *clobbered* [or *killed, murdered, destroyed*] that guy." Besides those idioms, we invent unique exaggerations daily: "Thanks for helping. You're the nicest person in Ohio."

We enjoy colorful exaggerations in our literature. Here the witty cop novelist Joseph Wambaugh has one of his characters describe a muscle-bound New Zealand World Cup sailor:

> "That humongous Kiwi next to her could pick his teeth with the bones of human cops," Forteny added. "Stretch that guy's T-shirt from bulkhead to bulkhead and it could sleep three."

Exaggeration, understood as such, is perfectly fine in informal speech and humorous writing. However, in serious discussions, it doesn't work. There, you should lean toward precision or even understatement, and away from over-statement. Compare these three expressions of the same sentiment:

Exaggeration:
The worst hypocrites in the world are vegetarians who wear leather gloves and fur-lined coats.

Precision:
Vegetarians who wear leather gloves and fur-lined coats are indirectly supporting the abuse of animals.

Understatement:
Vegetarians who wear leather gloves and fur-lined coats are not the lamb's best friend.

Even understatements can appear inappropriately informal or silly in serious contexts. Exaggeration is completely out of place. Without its humorous effect, exaggeration appears merely inaccurate. It has a desperate quality, as if you are trying to push your view dishonestly by inflating some element in your argument.

Closely related to the idea of avoiding exaggeration is the requirement for accuracy. Educated writers eschew large inaccuracies, such as the straw-man argument, which presents an exaggerated and unfair version of the opposing argument and then knocks it down. They are also fussy about details. They spell people's names correctly. They provide exact numbers when they are available. They don't write:

> There must have been at least a hundred snow days in Erie last year.

That sounds like wild guessing. They find out how many snow days there were and provide that number.

It is possible to make inaccurate statements by drawing conclusions on the basis of too little information or irrelevant information, as in these examples:

> I took a literature course from a professional novelist once. Professional writers make poor teachers.

> I can tell he's brainy by the way he looks and dresses.

You may, in fact, draw such tentative conclusions about people in your mind, as a practical strategy for getting on in life, but if you express such opinions in writing, you sound uneducated. Written conclusions should be based on stronger evidence.

Educated writers are careful that their words don't unintentionally overstate the case, as in this example:

> I credit Professor Smith's composition course with helping me master the art of writing and pass the freshman proficiency test.

Few people "master" anything as complex as writing. Most of us become "adequate" or "good" or "excellent" at the high-level skills we frequently use. Here is a more credible statement about this person's progress:

> I credit Professor Smith's composition course with helping me improve my writing significantly and pass the freshman proficiency test.

The above misuse of *master* is a problem of inadvertent exaggeration. It arises from a failure to pay attention to what one knows about the world and what constitutes accurate statements in terms of that knowledge. Test your assertions against your practical knowledge.

Many problems of inaccuracy arise simply from making statements that lack necessary qualifiers. Qualifiers are words and phrases that limit the implications of statements. Instead of saying or implying *all*, it is often more accurate to say *most, many*, or *some*. The second of these two statements is more accurate:

> In a run off, Nader supporters would vote for Gore, not Bush.

> In a run off, most Nader supporters would vote for Gore, not Bush.

Instead of saying or implying *always*, you may be more accurate saying *often* or *sometimes*. Again, the second of these two sample sentences is more accurate:

> Florida tourists head straight for the beach the moment they get settled in.

> Florida tourists often head straight for the beach the moment they get settled in.

Instead of saying or implying *everyone*, accuracy might require you to say *among those who* or *one of those who*, as in this example:

> Those who lose money in the stock market are "Johnny come lately" investors.

> Among those who lose money in the stock market are "Johnny come lately" investors.

Now that that point has sunk in, let's turn the principle around. It is possible to sound uneducated by overqualifying:

For most students, studying could lead to better grades.

For *most* students, studying *does* lead to better grades. Eliminate *could*:

For most students, studying leads to better grades.

Educated people get numbers right. This doesn't require being "good at math," just being commonsensical. The host of a TV political show, in an essay arguing against school distribution of condoms, wrote:

The worst of all this is the lie that condoms really protect against AIDS. The condom failure rate can be as high as 20 percent. Would you get on a plane—or put your children on a plane—if one in five passengers would be killed on the flight? Well, the statistic holds for condoms, folks.

No, the one-in-five death rate statistic doesn't hold for condoms. Common sense tells you that in order for a person to die of AIDS as a result of one sexual experience using a condom, all these conditions must be met:

1) the sexual partner must have AIDS (which is unlikely in this country)
2) the condom must fail (let's say a one in five chance)
3) the transference of fluids must then result in the contraction of AIDS (which occurs only rarely).

The mathematician John Paulos, in his book *Innumeracy: Mathematical Illiteracy and Its Consequences*, happens to cite some statistics on this issue. It turns out that the possibility of contracting AIDS from a single unprotected encounter (no condom) with a person you know has the disease is about 1 in 500. As long as your partner is not from a high-risk group such as drug needle users, if you use a condom when having sex with a person who may or may not have AIDS, the possibility of contracting the disease in one encounter is 1 in 50 million.

That's a lot different from 1 in 5.

Please do not use those figures as an excuse for unsafe sex. AIDS is more common now than when Paulos wrote his book, multiple encounters increase the odds, and AIDS is not the only risk. But do go away with a lesson about accuracy in numbers.

4-4 Fair-Minded versus Pushy

If you appear fair-minded—willing to consider the views of others—you will be more believable than if you merely thrust your opinions at your listener or reader. You are more likely to persuade if you appear to be a person of intellectual curiosity who carefully considers all aspects of a situation, than if you seem to be someone who self-righteously follows a narrow path with side blinders. Consider these two statements:

Pushy:

For those who are vegetarians for political reasons, the wearing of leather belts and fur-lined gloves is hypocritical. Those materials are obtained in the process of exploiting, even killing, animals. Vegetarians should stop wearing such clothing.

Fair-minded:

Those who are vegetarians for political reasons face a quandary when confronted with their use of leather belts and fur-lined gloves. One can make a reasonable argument that adult sheep can be sheared harmlessly, and therefore clothing lined with sheep fur is not exploitative, but many other farm-raised fur-bearing animals are raised in tiny cages and then slain to provide the silky linings and elegant exteriors of coats and gloves. Probably the best solution for political vegetarians is to vigorously seek out belts and lining made from synthetics. In the long run, this would create a greater market for such products, which in turn may draw even non-vegetarians away from animal skins.

Unsurprisingly, it takes more space to see a larger part of the picture. Note that the fair-minded voice is more interested in finding a solution to a problem than in rebuking others for doing something wrong. Where the assertive person sees a fault and assigns blame, the fair-minded person sees a problem and looks for a solution.

4-5 Idea Oriented versus Personal

In the example above, we saw the fair-minded person depersonalizing the discussion and focusing on ideas. Instead of calling the opponent a hypocrite, the fair-minded writer pondered the complexities of the issue. Attacking an opponent rather than that person's position on an issue is called making an "ad hominem argument" (ad = against; hominem = person). Ad hominem arguments are usually considered faulty logic. Such arguments can turn the discussion away from the real issues and raise the emotional level of the debate. Listen to this voice:

> Congressman Rapatio rants on and on about family values, while he himself keeps committing adultery, getting divorced, and marrying yet again. He should keep his mouth shut on the subject of morality.

And now this one:

> Congressman Rapatio, given his own record of adultery, is not the best spokesman for family values. But the real problem with his discussion of this issue is that he doesn't offer any ideas as to how government is supposed to salvage the traditional American family.

Indeed, the Congressman should probably "keep his mouth shut on the subject of morality," but that crudely stated assessment sounds less educated than the understated contention that he "is not the best spokesman for family values." Note that the second version, while mentioning the issue of character, which is probably legitimate in a political context, moves quickly away from that to "the real problem," the lack of substance in the Congressman's speeches.

John Allen Paulos, the mathematician mentioned earlier, argues that people who are ignorant about mathematics tend to personalize random or impersonal forces. Not understanding probability, they play their "lucky number" in the daily lottery, as if random selection had some mysterious connection to their street address, or whatever their lucky number is based on.

In a similar manner, writers who don't think like educated people personalize their discussions of social issues and problems. We're not talking here about personal anecdotes or stories, which can be an effective way to make a point by connecting it to real events. We're referring to a tendency to see the other side of an argument as a personal affront, followed by a tendency to claim a moral high ground above one's opponents in a debate. For example, to proceed as though the issue of abortion is not about when human life begins, but about who is a better person, the writer or those scoundrels who take the other side of the argument.

This kind of uneducated "reasoning" often ascribes unsavory motives to opponents, as in these two examples:

Those men in Congress who want to deprive a woman of control over her own body by banning abortions are trying to exercise the ancient dominance of males over females.

Abortion proponents are advocating murder for convenience. They argue that a woman who doesn't want to bear a child should be allowed to kill it.

A more educated approach would begin by assuming that most of those who oppose abortions sincerely believe that it amounts to the killing of an innocent child, and that most of those who support abortion don't believe that the process destroys an actual human being. With those assumptions in place, a writer on either side of the issue would be less inclined to use name calling and straw-man bashing and more inclined to use impersonal, rational methods of persuasion. A reasoned debate on abortion might center on what qualities define a human being and to what extent are those qualities present or missing in a fetus.

4-6 Cautious versus Certain

The worldly-wise writer has learned to avoid statements that express certainty about uncertain things. Compare these two statements:

Certain:
You should invest in the stock market. Stocks will continue to rise because the economy is basically sound.

Cautious:
Stock market investment is worth considering. Although the market is not entirely predictable, we can expect stocks to continue to rise because the economy is basically sound.

5

Incorporating Other Voices

Much of the writing you do in college will require you to react to something you have read, or to bring in the views of experts or the information those experts provide. For that reason, many composition programs teach you how to incorporate other voices and bring outside information into your short compositions. And most programs include a big research paper, which requires you to juggle perhaps eight or ten of these sources as you develop your own line of reasoning.

The effective incorporation of other voices and outside information into your own text is one of the most difficult aspects of academic writing. This subject is covered in traditional composition textbooks, and your instructor will probably have a lot to say about it, but it won't hurt to get another perspective from this book.

This chapter shows you when and how to summarize, paraphrase, and quote the words of others, and how to "document" those sources with notes and a bibliography. To document means to give credit to someone else for words or information or ideas, and to do so in such a way that readers can find the exact text or other source (such as a film) that you are drawing from. Readers may want to do that to further their own research into the subject.

As you bring other voices into your essay or report, it is important that you maintain your own voice as the dominant one. Don't just use your words to connect a series of summaries, paraphrases, and quotations.

Box 5-1 provides an example of an essay that draws from multiple sources and provides documentation of those sources. Note that the student writer's voice and purpose dominate, even though she draws on ideas and opinions from nine other writers in the course of her short essay.

Box 5-1 An Essay That Draws on Sources

A Beginner's Guide to Investment
By Yoshiko Maxwell

Before deciding whether to invest in stocks or bonds, you should understand the difference between saving money and investing it. Investment may not be appropriate for you. Saving is the putting aside of money for some purpose. Your purpose might be to buy some-thing—a vacation, an automobile, a new computer. Or you might save money as a hedge against unexpected events, such as getting laid off from your job or being faced with an emergency medical bill. By con-trast, an investment involves setting aside extra money you don't need in the foreseeable future, with an expectation of significant long term growth. Remember those key concepts: *money you don't need, long term*, and *significant growth*.

Savings should be kept in non-risk financial instruments, such as a bank savings account, a money market account, or a CD (Certified De-posit). CDs have a term constraint: you might buy a three month CD, a six month CD, a twelve month CD, or one with an even longer life.

Investment involves gambling, or risk-taking. Some people have a stronger stomach for gambling or a deeper pocket than others; they are the ones who are especially suited for taking risks with at least some of their money. As investment banker Ronald Marcus puts it, "Your tolerance for risk depends on many things: your age, your job security, your asset size, your life style, your family, and so on" (76). For example, if your job is secure and your retirement pension is a sure thing, you can afford to take more risks with extra money than can people whose circumstances are less solid.

Once you have decided to invest some of your extra money, you must decide whether to invest in stocks or bonds. Bonds are usually more secure, so let's start with them. When an entity (the federal government, a local government, a government agency, or a private corporation) wants to raise money, it can borrow from you and give you a promissory note to repay the loan, with interest, at some point in the future. The promissory note is called a bond. Since an issuer incurs a

continued

Box 5-1 An Essay That Draws on Sources *continued*

debt, this approach to raising money is called "debt financing." Interest rates vary. As bond expert Michael Perflink explains:

> If an issuer has good financial strength, it doesn't have to offer high interest rates because it can offer a safe investment for a bond purchaser. On the other hand, if an issuer has less financial stability, it has to offer higher interest rates to find people willing to lend it money by purchasing its bonds. Risky, high-interest corporate bonds are called "junk bonds." (87)

Corporations can also raise money by issuing stocks. Corporations don't issue a promissory note for stocks. Instead, purchasing stocks means that you own a part of the corporation. For corporations, this is called "equity financing," as opposed to debt financing. Instead of interest, corporations may give you dividends, a small part of the company's annual profit. Management decides how much of a dividend to issue. When you put your money in stocks, you have no certainty of getting the money back. If the corporation is successful, you may enjoy generous dividends and appreciation of stock value. Some investors select stocks that will provide good dividends. Others select stocks with the expectation that their value will go up sharply (appreciation). A young, growing company tends not to give dividends, but may appreciate quickly.

If you buy stocks from one company, your risk is high. You may lose your entire investment. You can reduce your risk by diversifying your investment, purchasing stocks from several companies instead of just one. Professional financial advisors strongly recommend diversification (Monroe; Peters and Shirwood; Londondale; Rohnert). You could further reduce your risk by investing in a huge number of companies, but to do that on your own would require a great deal of money, more than you may have available. But there's a solution to that—mutual funds. With mutual funds, many people contribute to a fund which is then used to buy an array of stocks. A manager of the fund gathers various stocks following a guideline which was set up at the inception of the fund. The guideline designates the types of stocks the manager is to purchase. For example, for quick appreciation, the fund may consist of stocks from only small companies. Or to cash in on appreciation from a growing sector, such as pharmaceuticals, the fund might purchase stocks from an assortment of drug companies. Or the fund might consist of a hybrid of stocks and bonds for balanced growth. The possibilities are numerous.

Investment consultant George Coltrain recommends mutual funds as the safest way to make a good return on your investment,

continued

Box 5-1 An Essay That Draws on Sources *continued*

"particularly if you invest in more than one fund" (22). Coltrain points out that you can create your own portfolio by mixing a selection of mutual funds and other investments. For a person of average tolerance of risk, Wall Street investment broker Jill Packard advises that you invest "40% of the portfolio in equity [stock] funds, 20% in International funds, 30% in bond funds, and 10% in a money market fund for liquidity" (D2). Packard adds, "Within that ratio guideline, you can diversify by buying a few funds in each category" (D2). Here again, the key to safety is diversification.

Securities companies used to be the only place you could buy and sell stocks. You paid a hefty commission whenever you bought or sold a stock, and in return the company gave you its expert advice. You can now trade on your own through the Internet, paying very small fees. You can also find free investment guidance on the Internet. For example, the Morning Star site (www.morningstar.com) can be very useful for your decision-making. Once you make up your portfolio, regularly monitor how it is doing, but don't rush to change it every week. That just costs you money. Remember, stocks are long term investments. A good general rule is to make an adjustment to your portfolio once every year or two (Goodman 45).

Works Cited

Coltrain, Mitzy B. "How Not to Lose Your Shirt in the Market." Home page. 6 Mar. 2000. 4 June 2002 <http://www.users.com/~mcoltrain/>.

Goodman, Drew. "Adjusting Your Portfolio." *Journal of American Business* 5.2 (1999): 145-49.

Londondale, Fritz M. "Bonds and Junk Bonds: Is There a Difference?" *U.S. Investment Journal* 45 (2001): 567-75.

Marcus, Ronald P. *Investment for Beginners*. New York: Manfield Publications, 1999.

Monroe, Hughes. "Methods of Professional Investors." *Business Practices Today*. Ed. Louise Dammitt and Marsha Trimbell. Boston: Haldman & Chrone Press, 1998. 401-08.

Packard, Jill. "Creating a Balanced Portfolio." *Hillsboro Herald* 20 Oct. 2000: D2.

Perflink, Michael. "Junk Bonds." *Investor Magazine* Apr. 2001: 87-90.

Peters, Stella, and Nancy Shirwood. *Making Money in the Market*. Pittsfield, OH: Hummingbird Publications, 2002.

Rohnert, Samuel. "Why Bonds Are Better In Hard Times." *Investment Research Online* 5.6 (2002): 3 pp. 4 Dec. 2002 <http://www.moneyonline.com>.

5-1 Summarizing

Summarizing means providing the gist of someone else's text in your own words. You might summarize a ten-page chapter in half a page, or a two-page passage in a paragraph.

You summarize for a purpose, usually to bring into your paper information and ideas relevant to the points you want to make about your subject. A summary, then, is not necessarily a balanced version of the other person's complete text. Instead, you leave out any material that is not relevant to your purpose and zero in on material that is relevant. In short, you usually summarize parts of a text, not the whole text.

Here's a three-step process for summarizing:

1. As you read the text, take notes on those points that are important to an issue in your essay, or highlight them with a highlighter or underline them.
2. Read over those points, ignoring the rest of the text. This puts an abbreviated, relevant version of the original text in your mind.
3. Put aside the text and your notes and write from memory and understanding, using your own phrasing.

When you go to write the summary, begin by naming the author and possibly the title of the text. Box 5-2 shows several ways to correctly structure this useful formulaic sentence, and several ways to do it wrong. Notice that when the sentence is structured correctly, either the author or the title is the subject of the verb. In the ungrammatical versions, a pronoun is the subject.

Continue to keep the reader informed as to whose views are being presented. Here's an example:

Jeff McQuillan, in his book *The Literacy Crisis: False Claims, Real Solutions*, reviews studies that conclude that access to books and certain types of support by parents and teachers lead to successful reading. Children who learn how to read on their own before

Box 5-2 First Sentence for Summaries

Possibility #1: Make the author the subject of the sentence

a) James Conant, in his essay "Athletics: The Poison Ivy in Our Schools," criticizes the emphasis placed on competitive athletics in our schools.

b) In his essay "Athletics: The Poison Ivy in Our Schools," James Conant criticizes the emphasis placed on competitive athletics in our schools.

Possibility #2: Make the title the subject of the sentence

c) "Athletics: The Poison Ivy in Our Schools," by James Conant, criticizes the emphasis placed on competitive athletics in our schools.

d) James Conant's "Athletics: The Poison Ivy in Our Schools" criticizes the emphasis placed on competitive athletics in our schools.

DO NOT USE A PRONOUN AS THE SUBJECT

Wrong:

e) In "Athletics: The Poison Ivy in Our Schools," by James Conant, he criticizes the emphasis placed on competitive athletics in our schools.

Wrong:

f) In James Conant's "Athletics: The Poison Ivy in Our Schools," he criticizes the emphasis placed on competitive athletics in our schools.

Wrong:

g) In "Athletics: The Poison Ivy in Our Schools," it criticizes the emphasis placed on competitive athletics in our schools.

---

school, according to McQuillan, do so without being pushed to read and without receiving formal instruction from their parents, though in most cases the parents read to their children. McQuillan also looks at efforts to teach reading at an early age and finds that such efforts have no lasting effect. He concludes that "access to print, not age, is the critical ingredient to achievement" (38).

Note the reference to the author in each of the four sentences:

> Jeff McQuillan . . . reviews
> . . . according to McQuillan . . .
> McQuillan also looks . . .
> He concludes . . .

That continual attribution makes it clear whose views are being expressed in this summary, namely the views of some other author, not yours (though you may agree with those views). This clarity becomes particularly important when you are bringing in statements from multiple authors. You have to keep the different voices clearly identified at all times through attributive statements like those above and these below:

> Martin says that . . .
> Jones believes that . . .
> In Smith's view . . . .

Note also that the author's full name may be used the first time (Jeff McQuillan reviews . . .), but only the last name is used in subsequent references (McQuillan also looks . . .). Some writers use only the last name, even on the first reference. Never refer to authors by their first name only.

5-2 Paraphrasing

A paraphrase is an almost line-by-line rendition of what an author said, interspersing your own phrasing with the author's. The author's words will appear inside quotation marks. Below is an original text and a paraphrase:

Original
Much of the writing you do in college will require you to react to something you have read, or to bring in the views of experts and the

information those experts provide. For that reason, many composition programs teach you how to incorporate other voices and bring outside information into your short compositions.

Paraphrase

In the first paragraph of his chapter "The Use of Sources," Murdick tells us that a lot of college writing "will require you to react to something you have read" or bring in information from those texts. Therefore, according to Murdick, it is common for composition programs to teach that skill.

Paraphrasing is not easy. It takes a flexibility with language that most composition students are still acquiring. When beginning writers try to present material this closely to the original, they often end up plagiarizing on the sentence level; that is, they end up using language too close to the original without using necessary quotation marks. Don't be discouraged from attempting paraphrasing. You aren't going to learn if you don't start trying. Just be aware of the potential problem. You don't want to paraphrase like this:

Original

Much of the writing you do in college will require you to react to something you have read or to bring in the views of experts and the information those experts provide.

Plagiarized attempt at paraphrase

According to Murdick, much of your college writing will require you to react to something you have read, or to bring in the viewpoints of experts and the information they provide.

The above example of paraphrase is too close to the original in phrasing:

Much of the writing you do in college
much of your college writing

will require you to react to something you have read
will require you to react to something you have read

or to bring in the views of experts
or to bring in the viewpoints of experts

and the information those experts provide
and the information they provide

The problem of avoiding the original phrasing is usually conquered by writing without looking at the original text. Unfortunately, to paraphrase, you have to look closely at the text in order to render its meaning line by line. Just be ready with the quotation marks. **If you can't avoid the original phrasing, don't try—use the unaltered original wording and put it in quotes.**

5-3 Quoting

Quotation marks are used to indicate that you are presenting someone's exact words. One of the worst mistakes beginning writers make is to put quotation marks around statements that inexactly represent what someone said or wrote. In short, to misquote. Quotation marks tell the reader that every word and every punctuation mark within the quotes is exactly as it appeared in the original (unless otherwise indicated; more about that below). Of course, if you are quoting what someone said, as opposed to wrote, you will have to supply the punctuation.

Uses of Quotations
Use quotations for purposes such as these:

- To bring in a statement that expresses an important thought particularly well

- To show indisputably that some authorities or published writers agree with your viewpoint
- To present, precisely, a view you disagree with so that you can reveal the weaknesses of that view
- To recognize where an original idea came from; to give credit
- To provide exact data and give credit to whoever first acquired it.

Providing Attributions

Never drop quotations into your text from out of the sky. Always introduce them by naming the speaker or writer. Here are some attributing phrases you can use for complete sentence quotations:

> According to Smith, "The present bull market is doomed."
> Smith says, "The present bull market is doomed."
> In Smith's words, "The present bull market is doomed."
> As Smith puts it, "The present bull market is doomed."

Notice, in the above examples, the comma after the initial attributing phrase. Note that the period at the end of each sentence goes to the left of the closing quotation mark. In American English, **periods and commas always go** *inside* **(to the left of) end quotes**: ". . . ," and ". . . ." If you see either punctuation mark outside (to the right of) the end quote in a published text, it means that that text was written in British English style. Even if you are a foreign student from Great Britain, you should follow American English conventions in your composition courses.

It is also possible to put the attributing phrase in the middle of the quoted sentence. Notice how that is punctuated:

> "The present bull market," according to Smith, "is doomed."

The word *is* is not capitalized because it is not the beginning of a new sentence. But observe how the quotation below is punctuated and how the first word of the second full sentence is capitalized:

> "The present bull market is doomed," according to Smith. "Furthermore, it won't revive soon."

Naming Titles

You may wish to name the work that you are drawing from, as well as the author, as in the next example. Naming the work characterizes the source. In the example, the source is a textbook, which has more authority than, say, a letter to the editor or an online listserv statement.

> Murdick and Bloemker, in their textbook *The Portable Technical Writer*, tell us that field testing documentation is "particularly useful for online documentation, which can be updated immediately after the test results have been analyzed" (240).

Identifying Authors

By identifying unknown authors you can establish their credentials, their authority to speak on a subject. For example:

> —Richard Rothstein, education columnist for the *New York Times*, reports that. . . .
> —According to Alisha Rixey, a financial consultant to non-profit organizations, the stock market. . . .
> —Computer programmer Mark Fields suggests that. . . .

Adding to, and Deleting from, Quotations

It is possible to add words and punctuation or delete them from quotations, but you must indicate that you are doing so. You might add a word to make the quotation comprehensible out of its original context:

> The President said, "I looked into his [Putin's] soul."

In the above example, the pronoun *his* is identified as *Putin's*. That would have been obvious from the original context, because other statements would have made it clear, but it isn't obvious out of context. Notice the use of square parentheses (called "brackets") to indicate to the reader that text is being added to the quotation. Do not use the regular round parentheses for this job.

You can delete words from quotations if they are unnecessary to your purpose and take up a lot of space:

Original full text
He noted that "our company has manufacturing plants in many places in the Northeast, including Albany, Philadelphia, Brooklyn, and Long Island, as well as a plant in Miami."

Quotation with deleted words
He noted that "our company has manufacturing plants in many places in the Northeast . . . as well as a plant in Miami."

Notice the use of three dots (called "ellipses") to indicate that words have been deleted from the original statement. If you end a sentence with ellipses, use four dots, the last one being the period.

Partial Sentence Quotations

You can also quote a part of a sentence:

Smith says that today's market "is doomed."

When using a partial-sentence quotation, be sure that your sentence is formed so that the quoted material fits in smoothly and grammatically.

Long Quotations

For long quotations that run more than three lines, do not use quotation marks. Instead, indent from the left:

In his book *The Portable Business Writer*, William Murdick makes this contrast:

> Experts in international communications have described in broad terms cultural differences important to communication. On the most general level, the United States, Israel, and the countries of northern Europe, especially Nordic countries and Germany, use similar rhetorics and ways of doing business. But countries in southern Europe, the Middle East, Asia, and Latin America differ in varying ways from the first group in regard to vital issues such as directness in communication and the importance of ritual. (70)

Murdick goes on to show how this contrast explains differences between Japanese and American business communications.

The "(70)" at the end of the long quotation is the page number in the text from which the quotation was taken. In short quotations, the page number goes to the right of the closing quotation marks but to the left—or inside—the period. However, as you can see in the example above, in long quotations, the page number goes to the right of the final period, outside the last sentence. Here's the contrast:

> . . . market "is doomed" (24). **[short quotation]**
> . . . importance of ritual. (70) **[long quotation]**

5-4 Documenting Sources: When to Do It

Documenting sources means telling the reader where you got your information or idea or quotation from. It is not always clear when you need to document and when you don't. Here are some guidelines:

1. **Give credit to your source for unique ideas, information, data, or words.** Unique means something that that source, and that source alone, created. You don't need to document that which is available from many sources. For example, the approximate population of the United States or the circumference of the

Earth are available from many sources. The same is true for a news event that is currently being described on the front page of most newspapers.

2. **When in doubt, name your source.** If you don't know if an idea or a piece of information is unique to the writer you got it from or widely known and mentioned by many, cite your source.

3. **Name your source if it would be helpful.** In some cases, even if the information you are introducing is not unique to your source, your readers might appreciate knowing where you got the information, in order to pursue the topic in more detail. If you think that might be the case, cite your source.

4. **List one or more sources to show that one or more authorities agree with you.** If you believe X, you may want to mention several published sources who also advance the X viewpoint, to show that you are not alone in believing X. This "appeal to authority" gives your viewpoint more credibility. The essay in Box 5-1, for example, contains this sentence:

> Professional financial advisors strongly recommend diversification (Monroe; Peters and Shirwood; Londondale; Rohnert).

Those names in parentheses are sources—experts—who strongly recommend diversification in stock investment.

5. **List sources to prove that what you are saying is true or accurate.** At the end of the essay in Box 5-1, the reader will be able to find Monroe, Peters and Shirwood, Londondale, and Rohnert in a list of sources entitled "Works Cited." There, the reader will learn the titles of the texts in which these cited authors made their recommendation for diversity in investment. Your citation, in effect, provides evidence that what you are saying is true, evidence the reader can examine by going to your sources and checking them out.

5-5 Documenting Sources: How to Do It

The process of documenting a source requires two steps. You need an in-text signal or note to indicate that you are documenting a statement or a quotation, and then you need an end-of-text bibliographical statement which provides information about the source, such as the title of the article you are quoting from and what journal it appeared in. Both in-text parenthetical notes and a bibliography entitled Works Cited appear in the model essay in Box 5-1. You might want to take a quick look at Box 5-1 (p. 72) before reading on.

Just stating an author's name can be enough of a signal that you are citing someone and that there will be a bibliographical entry for this person. For example:

> Nathaniel Lassitur, a New York vintner, believes that satellite photography can make our wine growing better than Europe's.

From that sentence, the reader can assume that in the bibliography at the end of the essay the name **Lassitur, Nathaniel** will appear, and after that name will be the title of the text that Lassitur wrote in which he expressed his views about satellite photography.

In the above case, the writer is citing a general belief on the part of an author, not something specifically stated on a particular page. Most of the time, however, you will be referring to something specifically stated, in which case you should locate that statement by putting the page number or numbers in a parenthetical note:

> Lassitur wants NASA to provide American vintners with photographs of their crops for free, "since we pay for NASA with our tax dollars" (23).

If the quotation runs from one page to the next in the original text, you include the range of pages: (23-24).

An in-text parenthetical note is a clear signal to the reader that there is an end-of-text bibliographical statement which provides full information on the source. Decades ago it was common for the bibliographical statement to appear at the bottom of the page as a footnote, but nowadays scholars and report writers usually put this information at the end of the text, in a list of sources, called generically a "bibliography." Different professional associations use different titles for their bibliographies. The Modern Language Association (MLA) uses the phrase "Works Cited," while the American Psychological Association (APA) uses the term "References."

Various professional organizations have their own ways of formatting in-text notes and end-of-text bibliographies. Let's look at two of them, to see the contrast. MLA style, developed by the Modern Language Association, is used by students and scholars in English, foreign languages, and other humanities. The second example below, APA style, developed by the American Psychological Association, is used by those in psychology and other social sciences, including education. There are also specific styles for various hard sciences, such as chemistry and biology. Here is what an in-text, parenthetical note looks like in MLA and APA:

MLA Style in-text, parenthetical note:

The Japanese in particular "abhor rudeness and explicit confrontation" (Murdick 77).

APA Style in-text, parenthetical note:

The Japanese in particular "abhor rudeness and explicit confrontation" (Murdick, 1999, p. 77).

In those examples, Murdick is the author. The numeral 77 is the page number the quotation comes from. And 1999 is the date of the publication of the text the quotation comes from. You may have noticed that APA style provides more information than MLA style, in particular the date. "Name-date" systems of documentation are quite popular in scholarly circles today. However, in a composition class taught by the English department, you may be required to use MLA style, which is not a name-date system.

Here's what a bibliographical entry looks like for each of those in-text notes:

MLA Style bibliography entry:

> Murdick, William. *The Portable Business Writer*. Boston: Houghton Mifflin, 1999.

APA Style bibliography entry:

> Murdick, W. (1999). *The portable business writer*. Boston: Houghton Mifflin.

Note the odd indentation in both cases, the opposite of a normal paragraph. That is called "hanging paragraph" style. It makes finding a name in a long alphabetical list easier than regular paragraph indentation or a block style with no indentation. In hanging paragraph style, the author's last name sticks out to the left, clearly visible (see the Works Cited at the end of the essay in Box 5-1).

5-6 MLA In-text Parenthetical Notes

If your composition instructor requires documentation of sources for your essays, that instructor will almost certainly teach the subject, and you will probably be required to purchase a textbook which provides complete details. This chapter will provide an explanation of the concepts, rather than a complete set of information about documentation. Complete information can be found in any English handbook or on the Web. To find appropriate information on the Web, do a search for "MLA style documentation." You'll find that many colleges publish MLA guides; you can pick and choose among them.

The explanations that follow should help you understand what your instructor or your handbook or your MLA Web site is saying about this subject. We'll stick with MLA style, since that is probably the style your instructor will prefer.

You saw examples of parenthetical documentation in the previous section. For MLA style, it consisted of simply the page number or the author's last name, a space, and a page number, all within parentheses, before the final period of the sentence. So, what's the problem? Well, it turns out that there are a number of commonly occurring situations that require you to do slightly different things in the course of providing proper parenthetical documentation. Here are some of them:

Two or More Authors

If the authors' names don't appear in your text, put them in the parenthetical note with the word *and* between them, like this:

> However, it should be pointed out that "nonlinear texts put a burden on readers to create their own sense of organization, sometimes leading to confusion" (Murdick and Bloemker 223).

When you get up to four or more authors, you stop listing them and state only the last name of the first of the authors (the name that appears first in the published text and the one that will appear first in your bibliography), followed by the expression "et al.," followed by the page number(s). The *et* part is Latin for "and"; *al.* is an abbreviation for a Latin expression meaning "all the others." In effect, the whole phrase means: "and all the rest of the authors." Here's an example:

> Few of those companies showed a profit in 1998 despite growing sales (Murray et al. 156-57).

A Moral Lesson about Details

Do you remember what each part of "et al." means? Or did your eyes glaze over when the discussion turned to Latin. Did you notice that the "al." part is an abbreviation and therefore requires a period after it, but the "et" part is not? Or do you routinely overlook such details because they bore you.

Documentation requires attention to detail. It is *all* detail. The details bring order to what would otherwise be an immense chaos, and you will come to appreciate that order as you progress through college.

You don't have to memorize all the formats, but you should have a general sense of what's going on, of what the problems are that need to be solved in some manner or other. For example, what do you do if the text you are quoting from has no named author? Or what do you do if the author is not a person but some organization, such as your college? You don't need to memorize what to do in such instances, but you should be aware that problems like those arise, and you should know that there are answers in your handbook or on the Web.

Everyone groans inwardly when dealing with the interminable details of documentation. You are not alone in that feeling. But there's no profit in being a big baby about it. After all, it's not as hard as learning how to drive a car. If all those crazies out there on the highway can somehow earn a driver's license, you can surely get a handle on MLA documentation.

Formatting Page Number Ranges

Note how ranges of page numbers are formatted in MLA style:

    . . . our tax dollars (23-24).
    . . . despite growning sales (Murray et al. 156-57).

In the second example, instead of 156-157, just the 57 appears. In presenting page numbers and years, *don't repeat* numerals representing hundreds or thousands. Write 123-24 and 1354-65. However, if your page sequence runs from 299 to 304, then you have to write 299-304, because the hundreds numeral is not *repeated*; it changes from 2 to 3.

Do repeat numerals representing tens: 21-23. The 2 represents the number of tens in the number (2 of them), so you repeat it.

Naming Authors in the Text

In most of our examples of parenthetical notes so far, the author's name has appeared inside the parenthetical note. However, unless it is inconvenient to do so, it is better to name the author(s) in your text, like this:

> Murdick and Bloemker point out that "nonlinear texts put a burden on readers to create their own sense of organization, sometimes leading to confusion" (223).

Notice that the names are not repeated in the parenthetical note. That's because the reader knows who the authors are from the text. You put the least amount of necessary information in the parenthetical note. The page number for the quotation must go in, because that will not appear in the Works Cited entry. The reader knows where to look in the Works Cited to find this text—under Murdick and Bloemker.

Unknown and Organizational Authors

If the author is unknown, the work will be listed in the Works Cited by its title. So mention the title in the text:

> The book *Recipes*, published during the Civil War, suggests that meat was served sparingly in those days.

In the case of an organizational author, name the organization:

> The Baskinski Corporation reports a loss in the third quarter of this year (23).

More Than One Work by the Same Author

In a long report, you may find yourself drawing on more than one article or book by the same expert. This would be quite common, since most experts write often about the same subject. Those writing on your subject probably have a number of publications that you can learn from.

If multiple works by the same author appear in your bibliography, distinguish among those works in the text by mentioning the title of the work you are presently drawing from:

> Rupert Jones, in "The Art of Sailing," describes the kind of person who would "enjoy the sailing life" (12).

Or, you can put an abbreviated title inside the parenthetical note, consisting of the first word or two from the title:

> Rupert Jones describes the kind of person who would "enjoy the sailing life" ("The Art" 12).

Either approach allows the reader to distinguish among multiple *Jones* entries in the Works Cited.

5-7 The MLA Works Cited

The Works Cited comes at the end of your paper, beginning on a page of its own. If there is only one work in your Works Cited and you can fit it on the last page of your essay, your instructor will probably allow that. In such a case, title your bibliography Work Cited, not Works Cited.

General Format

The entries in a Works Cited are listed in alphabetical order by the last name of the author or the first word of the title if there is no author. When alphabetizing by title, don't count the articles *the* and *a/an* as words; use the first word beyond them. Box 5-1 includes a Works Cited, which you can use as a model when you go to create your own bibliography. It contains examples of the most common sources used by composition students. Each of those sources is discussed below.

If you find that you are using a type of source which is not explained below, then you can find an explanation, or at least a model for that type of entry, on the Web or in an English handbook.

The Works Cited should be double-spaced like the rest of the paper. Do not put an extra blank line between entries. Be careful about spelling the names of people, organizations, publishers, and places. Your spell checker will not distinguish between correctly and incorrectly spelled names. Remember from Chapter 4: The educated voice is accurate.

When you are listing more than one work by the same author, you do not repeat the author's name. Instead, after the first work, you put three hyphens and a period:

> Gatsby, Marsha. "Election Fraud in Florida: 1980-2000." *The Journal of American Politics* 87 (2001): 452-67.
> ---. "The Psychological Difficulties Inherent in Butterfly Ballot Designs." *American History Quarterly* 93 (2001): 366-78.

Works by the same author should be alphabetized by the titles of the works (ignoring *The* and *A/An*). In the above example, the words *Election* and *Psychological* were used to determine which entry came first.

Capitalizing Words in the Titles of Works

Titles of works follow these two rules for capitalization of words: (1) Capitalize the first word of titles and subtitles, and (2) capitalize all other words except articles (*the, a, an*), prepositions (*of, for,* etc.), and coordinating conjunctions (*and, but, or,* etc.).

When there is a subtitle, the main title ends with a colon (:) and the subtitle follows, as in this example:

> The Heroics of Lewis and Clark: A Lesson for Us All

Note in the example above that the words *The* and *A* are capitalized because they are the first words of the title and subtitle; otherwise they would not be.

Italics and Quotation Marks

Quotation marks go around the titles of short works, such as essays, newspaper articles, magazine articles, chapters in books, poems and short stories, and songs:

> According to the article "Bonds and Junk Bonds: No Big Difference," all bond purchases operate on the same principles.

Do not put quotation marks around the title of your own essay when it appears at the top of the first page or on a separate title page. However, in the unlikely event that you were to mention your own title in the body of your text, you would put quotation marks around it.

Italics are used for the titles of long works, such as books, movies, and record albums: *The Portable Technical Writer / A Beautiful Mind.*

Italics are also used for the names of publications, such as newspapers, magazines, and journals: the *New York Times / Newsweek / Rhetoric Review.* Note that, by tradition, the word *the* is not capitalized or italicized, even if it is a part of the actual name of the periodical (as in the case of the *New York Times*).

Abbreviation of Months

MLA style abbreviates most months in Works Cited entries: *Jan.* instead of January. Keep months down to four letters or fewer: Jan., Feb., Mar., Apr., May, June, July, Aug., Sept., Oct., Nov., Dec.

Information Required for Works Cited Entries

The general content for Works Cited entries is as follows. For books, you insert

1. the author(s)
2. the title of the book, including edition number
3. the place of publication
4. the publishing company
5. the date of publication.

For articles in a magazine, journal, or newspaper, you insert:

1. the author(s)
2. the title of the article
3. the name of the publication
4. volume/edition and date information
5. page numbers for the article.

When taking notes during the research process, number the citation information as above (1-5) to make sure that you have recorded all necessary information. Then for each note, ask yourself: Do I have five distinct pieces of information?

Online sources require different sets of information depending on the type of source.

Below is a description and discussion of the seven sources you will most likely use: book, anthology, newspaper, magazine, scholarly journal, Web site, and online journal.

Book

Applebee, Helen, and Susan Martin. *Florida Election Law.* New York: Landon & Sons, 1998.

The first author's name is entered last-name-first (Applebee, Helen). This helps the reader find a particular author in the alphabetized list. The second author's name is entered first-name-first (Susan Martin), because there is no advantage there to reversing name order. New York is the place of publication. You can find that at the beginning of the book, usually on the title page. Dig around for it if necessary. If more than one city appears, use the first one mentioned. If you see more than one date at the front of the book, pick the latest.

If you are citing an essay collection but not any particular essay in the book, then the editors' names would appear at the outset, in the same location as if they were authors, except the abbreviation "ed." would appear after the name:

> Withspoon, Mildred, ed. *The Southern Voices Collection*. 2nd ed. Boston: McFee, 1990.

In the case of multiple editors, use "eds.":

> Smith, Ronald P., and Suzanne Morehouse, eds. *An Anthology of Canadian Poetry*. New York: Mt. Pontiflier Press, 1997.

Essay in an Anthology

> Barach, Martin J. "From Palm Beach to Tallahassee: The Fight for Florida." *The 2000 Election Fiasco*. Ed. James Dubois and Mark Ridge. San Francisco: U of the West P, 2002. 9-18.

Martin Barach wrote the article "From Palm Beach to Tallahassee: The Fight for Florida" that you read in the book *The 2000 Election Fiasco*. His name would appear in the parenthetical note in your text (not the editors' names, James Dubois and Mark Ridge). The article title has quotation marks around it, with the final period going inside (that is, to the left of) the closing quotes. The title of the book in which the article or chapter appeared is written in italics. *Ed.* stands for "edited by." (Even if there are two editors, don't write "Eds." in this situation.) The letters *U* and *P* stand for "University" and "Press."

Article in a Newspaper

Author named

> Dunbar, Kathy. "The Role of Katherine Harris in the Florida Mess." *Wakulla Beach Bugle* 23 Jan. 2001: B3+.

Author not named
"Ernest Effort at Election Reform Fails." *New York Times* 14 Aug.
    2001, natl. ed.: A2-3.

In the first example, the city or town is named in the
newspaper's title: Wakulla Beach. If the newspaper's name
were simply *The Bugle*, you would do this:

Dunbar, Kathy. "The Role of Katherine Harris in the Florida Mess."
    Bugle 23 [Wakulla Beach, FL] Jan. 2001: B3+.

The publication location for the newspaper now appears
after the name, with square brackets around it. The words
The and *A* are always omitted from the name of a newspaper
in a citation. So *The Wakulla Beach Bugle* becomes *Wakulla
Beach Bugle*, and *The Bugle* becomes *Bugle*.

Note that dates are written with the day first, month second: 23 Jan. and 14 Aug. (This is the opposite of what we
normally do: Jan. 23.) Looking at the first example, "B3"
means page 3 of section B. The plus sign means that the
article continues on another page deeper in the section. If it
continued on the next page, you would indicate that, as in
the second example: A2-3. The section indicator, A, is not
repeated, since newspaper articles never extend from one
section of the newspaper to another.

In the second example, the edition is included: natl. ed.
(national edition). The *New York Times* also issues both an
early and a late local edition, as do many newspapers. Late
editions are different from early editions. If the edition is
named in the newspaper's masthead, indicate the edition
with the words "late ed." or "early ed." or "natl. ed." or whatever expression appears in the banner.

Editorial in a Newspaper
"The Fight for Election Reform." Editorial. *Carabelle Tribune* 2 June
    2001: B2.

Unsigned articles and editorials are listed by their titles, in alphabetical order, ignoring *The* and *A/An*. In the example above, the first word of the title is *Fight,* once you eliminate *The,* so you would use *Fight* to place the article alphabetically in your Works Cited list.

Article in a Magazine

Carpenter, Margaret. "Who Stole the Election?" *Public Forum* 18 Dec. 2000: 12-16.

If the magazine comes out more than once a month, include the day of the month that the particular issue you are citing was published; in the example, that would be 18. If the magazine is a monthly, leave out the day and just put in the month and year. In either case, end with the page numbers of the article. Include a + sign if the text skips pages: 6-7+.

To review, the titles of short works, such as articles, have quotation marks around them ("Who Stole the Election?"). The names of magazines, journals, and newspapers go in italics. In the example above, *Public Forum* is the name of a magazine.

Article in a Scholarly Journal

With continuous pagination

Gatsby, Marsha. "Election Fraud in Florida: 1980-2000." *The Journal of American Politics* 87 (2001): 452-68.

Without continuous pagination

Gibbons, Ralph S. "Were Black Voters Cheated in Florida?" *Poly Sci* 45.2 (2001): 34-46.

When you create a Works Cited entry for a magazine, you name the month (see the example in the previous section; the month of publication, Dec., is named). With a journal, you don't name the month. Instead, you indicate the volume number and possibly the issue number. The volume is the set of issues that came out during a particular year. If a journal began its existence in 1970, then volume 1 for that journal would be 1970, volume 2 would be 1971, and so forth. Journals usually publish two to four issues per year. In the first example above, 87 is the volume number and 2001 is the year that volume 87 came out. The numerals 452-68 mean that the article ran from page 452 through 468.

The second example provides both the volume number, which is 45, and the issue number, which is 2. The volume and issue numbers are written with a decimal point between them: 45.2. To find the article, you would get the 2nd issue of volume 45. The first entry doesn't require the issue number because it uses "continuous pagination" throughout the volume. In other words, if the first issue is 187 pages long, the second issue begins with page 188, not page 1, and so forth throughout the year. Since the page number is given, you don't need the issue number to find the right issue; you just find the issue that has the desired pages. You can't do that in a journal that starts every issue with page 1 (non-continuous pagination) because every issue will have, for example, pages 34-46. If a journal has continuous pagination, only the first issue will have pages 34-46.

How do you know if a journal has continuous pagination (you don't put in the issue number) or non-continuous pagination (you do put in the issue number)? If the page numbers for the article are very high, in the 400s say, you can safely assume continuous pagination. Otherwise, you'll have to look at an issue later than the first to see if it starts with page 1 or a higher page number.

Is this a ridiculous pain? Wouldn't it be easier for both you and the reader if you always put in the issue number? Perhaps. But if you're working on a research paper, don't distract yourself by fretting over petty inconveniences. Put up with them and get on with the job. When the term is over, you can amuse yourself by writing a complaint letter to the Modern Language Association.

Article from a Web Site

Personal site

Gergen, Mathew. "Recount Silliness." Home page. 8 Nov. 2000.
7 Oct 2001. <http://www.users.com/~gmathew/>.

Professional site

"Recount Inconsistencies." Political News Network. 12 March 2001.
<http://www.politicalnews.com>.

The first example above is a personal Web site, meaning it belongs to a person rather than an organization or a business. It has no name, so the term *Home Page* is inserted. If the personal site does have a name, such as "Pam's Corner," put in that name instead of "Home Page." The first date is the date the article was posted (if such a date is given). The second is the date of retrieval, the day you went to that site and found the source. If you went to the site several times, put in the date of your latest visit when the article was still there.

In the second example, we have a professional site called *Political News Network.* There is no publication date available. When there is only one date, it is the retrieval date.

Article from an Online Journal

Magilliver, Norman. "Ballot Reform Efforts." *The Journal of Florida Politics* 4.2 (2001): 11 pp. 22 Mar. 2002 <http://www. flapolitics. com>.

Note the conventional presentation of the volume and issue number (4.2). The date of publication appears in parentheses: (2001). In the case of online publications, always include the issue number.

After the year of publication, indicate the range of pages, if that appears, such as **42-56**. If the pages for all articles are numbered starting with 1, indicate the number of pages, such as: **12 pp.** If there are no page numbers, but paragraphs are numbered, put in the number of paragraphs, such as: **12 pars**.

If nothing is numbered, put in nothing. Instead, replace the colon after the publication year with a period and move on to the date of retrieval. For example: **4.2 (2001). 22 Mar 2002**.

The Modern Language Association provides a three-page list of examples of different types of Works Cited entries for Web sources. At the time of this writing, the list was available through the following set of links. Go to the MLA Web site at **www.mla.org**. Click on **MLA Style**, then **Frequently Asked Questions**, then **How do I document sources from the World Wide Web in my works-cited list?**

5-8 The Reliability of Sources

Magazines and journals are different kinds of publications. One obvious difference is that you can buy a printed magazine in a supermarket or book store, but you usually have to get a printed journal through subscription. College libraries subscribe to them, which means they are available to you for your research. Journals are produced by scholars for other scholars. These publications are used to disseminate research results and to discuss issues and developments within disciplines of study. Magazines, on the other hand, are produced for a general audience for enjoyment and information.

Journals tend to be more serious-minded than magazines, and more reliable. They are also more useful for extending your research. Most magazine articles will not have a Works Cited, since they are not based on library research or because the author feels no obligation to review the published research on the topic. Journal articles almost always have a Works Cited because scholarly research normally requires a review of relevant research and opinion. As you pursue your research projects in college, you will find that research reviews, and the bibliographies they produce, are very useful resources that alert you to texts relevant to your interests.

For some topics, your instructor may not allow you to use magazines as sources on the grounds that they are not intellectual enough or not reliable enough. Articles in "peer reviewed" journals have been examined by a group of experts to make sure that they make sense and that any inaccuracies are eliminated. Even journals that don't use a peer review process tend to be reliable sources, because the editors and others on the staff are experts in the general subject area. Magazines have varying degrees of reliability. A news magazine like *Time* or *Newsweek* might be a good source for an essay on gun control, but a magazine with a name like *Bullet World* or *Pacifist Weekly* would not be. Advocacy magazines are more interested in getting their views across than in checking the facts in the articles they publish.

Articles published on personal Web sites can be useful for providing interesting ideas about your topic, but you should be cautious about drawing information from such publications. There is no outside review of the information in these articles, not even by an editor. They are self-published. Articles published on professional Web sites may or may not offer reliable information, depending on the organization. Government Web sites, for example, are reliable sources; the sites of advocacy groups, such as www.SaveAmerica.com, are not.

Online versions of established print journals are reliable. Online journals that have no established print version should be examined closely for reliability. The editor should be a well-known expert in the field (do a Web search of the editor's name and read his or her resume). Peer reviewers, if there are any, should be listed. As with all sources, use caution and good judgment.

Part III

Handling the Major Assignments

This section describes the five most common writing assignments in composition today: the personal narrative, the informative article, the argument on a controversial issue, the literary criticism essay, and the long research paper. It provides content and structural options for creating a well-developed first draft for each kind of essay.

6

The Personal Narrative

Basic purpose is to tell a story

A narrative recounts a series of events, as in a story. A personal narrative recounts events in your life. Your composition instructor may ask you to write an essay about some important person or event in your life. This chapter shows you how to take a personal story and turn it into an essay.

Even if you are writing more about another person than about yourself—a character study of a favorite aunt, let's say—the principles below apply.

6-1 Outline for a Personal Narrative Essay

Another term for the personal narrative essay is "memoir." The memoir is a type of essay. How does one turn the recounting of an autobiographical episode into an essay? Writer Judith Barrington, in her book *Writing the Memoir: From Truth to Art*, answers that question this way:

> Rather than simply telling a story from her life, the memoirist both tells the story and muses upon it, trying to unravel what it means in the light of her current knowledge.

Barrington's definition of the memoir suggests the basic ingredients for this kind of essay: story telling and commentary. Here is a simple outline for writing a memoir, or meaningful personal narrative:

Memoir - story telling and personal commentary

1. Background *to setting where the events/episodes take place*
2. Episode *verbal, physical action & description*
3. Commentary.

Those elements do not have to come in that order. You can mix elements of background into the other two parts. You can begin with the episode, and then interrupt it with background or commentary. The order presented above is a logical one that you might use for a first draft of a personal-narrative composition. The model essay in Box 6-1 illustrates that organizational plan. The next section provides detail about each of these components.

Box 6-1   A Narrative Essay

Untitled essay by Traci E. Augustosky. From *Comp Tales*, edited by Richard H. Haswell and Min-Zhan Lu, Longman (2000). Reprinted with permission. Title added.

The Best Laid Plans
by
Traci E. Augustosky

Background

I had just started working for the local community college as a composition instructor when the department coordinator called me for a new assignment. The local sheriff's office had contracted the school to provide a few remedial writing courses for its employees. I happily accepted the appointment, firmly believing that non-traditional (i.e., old) students were the most motivated, cooperative, and rewarding. I composed a syllabus by mapping out a plethora of homework assignments, quizzes, and essays.

continued

Box 6-1   A Narrative Essay *continued*

The first day of class I walked into a silent room and looked out from a wobbly podium at a room full of stern faces and piercing eyes. My nervousness was exacerbated by the realization that not only were all of my new students clearly unhappy, but they were all in uniform and fully armed. I hesitantly handed out the syllabi and began to go over the course expectations and requirements. Each sentence I spoke seemed to elicit more animosity. Some of the students never unlocked their hard stare from me, never glanced once at the syllabi in front of them.

I stopped mid-sentence, pulled out a chair, plopped down in it in front of the podium, and looked at all of the deputies in the room. One man, sitting in the front row, slowly crossed one leg over the other, resting his ankle on the opposite knee. While conducting this performance for my benefit, he hiked up his pant leg just enough to expose the small firearm strapped underneath.

I simply asked, "What's going on here?"

After a few minutes of discussion, I discovered that the sheriff's office had forced all employees to take a placement test. Those students who received low scores were subsequently required to attend courses. Furthermore, this class was the group of students who had performed the lowest. They knew it. Their colleagues knew it. Their supervisors knew it. Their subordinates knew it. Unfortunately, until that very moment, their teacher had not.

I stood up, collected the course syllabi, and chucked them in the trash. We spent the remainder of the class discussing what they wanted to accomplish, what realistic goals we could set, what kind of time limitations they had in and out of the classroom, and what would encourage them to leave their side arms at home.

I learned a valuable lesson about the necessity of teacher adaptability. My idealistic notions of educational outcomes collided with the reality of classroom and student circumstances. By devising a plan that fit the circumstances, we were all able to reach the goals we set and still retain a modicum of pleasantness throughout the course. All students passed the placement exam when they re-took it at the end of the quarter, and I don't think I have to worry about getting a speeding ticket again as long as I live in this county (I'm just kidding, Sheriff).

Margin labels: scene · background · scene | Episode · Commentary

6-2 The Elements of a Narrative

Broad background is historical. It encompasses strangers, people other than the writer and the principal characters. It creates an historical setting for the story. A writer might begin a narrative about her experiences with a favorite grandparent of Italian descent by saying:

> In the 1890s, almost half the village of Dorfino in southeast Italy emigrated to the United States. The men were masons and established themselves in New Jersey. The women were homemakers who cooked the food from their native country. One of the first children to be born in the U.S within this immigrant community was a slender, pretty girl named Lucia Manchino, my grandmother.

Background is the setting things take place in

You may not need this kind of historical element in your narrative, but you should be aware of it as a possibility. **Focused background** introduces the characters of the narrative and brings us closer to the events that will dominate the memoir. In the above case, the focused narrative would begin as the writer concentrated on the life of Lucia.

An **episode** is the depiction of a specific event in the life of the writer (though, again, the focus may be on another character, the writer merely an observer or historian). It includes verbal action (dialogue) and physical action. It is often imbued with physical description so that the reader can "see" the action. The episode consists of one or more **scenes**. Think of a scene as what you would see and hear standing in one place at one specific period of time, while verbal or physical action occurs around you. The scene (or series of scenes) leads up to the episode's **climax**, in which something dramatic or important happens.

make sense

Commentary consists of the writer's attempt to understand the meaning of the episode and to explain that meaning to the reader. You can make such comments at any time:

rising action mounting situation point of climax resolution
background → becoming heated

before the episode, in the middle of it, or after it is over. In one common type of commentary, the writer reveals a sudden understanding of something right after the final climax. That unraveling of the "meaning of it all" is called the **denouement** (pronounced: *day-new-mon*).

denouncement

6-3 Bringing Your Narrative Alive

Your narrative will seem real and will hold your reader's interest if you alternate description and action.

Description

Describe so the readers will see your scenes and the action of characters as *you want* them to. Describe, in other words, to interfere with the readers' tendency to supply their own images from their own experience and imagination.

Often, you don't care how the readers see something, so leave it to them to create their own picture. In other words, don't describe every setting or every person in your story. Your narrative will move too slowly and will have no focus. Write "The teenaged pop vendor at the game almost spilled a cup of Coke Cola on Gina's lap, but her arms shot up and her own quick hands saved her from that soaking." That tells us something about Gina, her nimbleness. Don't weaken your focus by describing the Coke vendor in detail. That would be a distraction. It doesn't matter what the Coke vender looked like.

Once you've decided to describe something, be picky. Try to choose elements of a scene or a person that characterize. Suppose, for example, you grew up in a very strict household. Your parents kept tight control over your life and you were not allowed to wear certain clothes and do certain things that most other kids were allowed. You might describe your house physically as always being perfectly neat, never an open magazine on the coffee table, never the remains of lunch on the kitchen table, never a toothpaste tube squeezed from the top, never an unmade bed. Such a description would introduce an atmosphere of strict discipline. It would reflect the obsessive order and control your parents tried to impose on their world—and on you.

One way to prevent slowing your narrative with heavy description is to spread out the description over several passages. Provide some description of a main character at the beginning; then add some details in the middle of the narrative. You don't have to say everything at once. Connect pieces of description to the actions of the moment. As background, you might describe Gina as a tall, athletic, dark-haired 20-year-old. Later, you might focus in on certain details, perhaps describing her bright, eager eyes as she leans towards you across a table in a restaurant.

Actions *display character*

The actions of your characters create the plot, the shape, of your story. But they should also serve to reveal character. Think of the actions of important people in your narrative as *behavior*. General behavior is what you do habitually. Specific behavior is what you do in an unusual situation, because you are you.

In describing general behavior, you frequently use adverbs like *usually* and *often* and the auxiliary verb *would*:

> When my brother and I were young, we **often** spent our summer weekends accompanying our parents to tennis tournaments around upstate New York. As they played singles and mixed doubles matches, we **usually** played in the surrounding pine forests. I loved the woods, with their soft pine needles, their leafy smells, their shadows. I **would** be responsible for my little brother, Mark, and **would** make up games for us in which we played the roles of colonial explorers or Indians.

Creating action

Specific behavior takes place on one occasion. It creates an episode. The auxiliary verb *would* disappears as the writer begins to describe a unique event:

One weekend, Mark and I were playing on a hillside. I led him up the hill away from the tennis club, which we could see occasionally between the trees as we walked. Eventually, however, we were out of sight of civilization. I pressed on, wanting to see what was over the top of the hill. Mark was somewhere behind me as I made the crest and looked down the other side. There, not twenty feet down the other side, was a black bear routing its nose in some bushes. It stopped, turned its head, and looked at me. My fantasy about being an Indian warrior vanished. I thought of my little brother. How was I going to get him out of this?

I slunk backward, until I could no longer see the bear, then turned and dashed down the hill. But Mark wasn't there! I wanted to keep on running, get down to the tennis club and get help from the adults. But I couldn't leave Mark behind. I forced myself to stop, grabbing a tree trunk. I fearfully looked back toward the crest. There, far off to the left, was Mark, slowly making his way toward the top of the hill. I didn't want to yell, afraid that it would attract the bear. I didn't want to head back up, either, but I had to. I began running as fast and silently as I could toward Mark, trying to reach him before he came into the bear's sight. "Mark!" I whispered as loudly as I dared. "Mark! Mark!" Just before he reached the peak, he turned toward me, waited. I reached him and pulled him to my chest, gave him the *Shhh!* sign, and looked over his head for the bear.

Several aspects of the narrator's character are being revealed by these actions: his practicality, despite his love of fantasizing; the depth of his concern for his brother; his courage and ability to act in a crisis. The story will become particularly powerful if, at the end, the narrator reveals that he learned something from this adventure, perhaps something about the dangerousness of the world, despite its beauty, or something about his attachment to his brother, one that is stronger than his attachment to his parents. That revelation would come in a final commentary.

Verbal action, or dialogue, is more common in fiction than in non-fiction personal narratives. Use dialogue sparingly, but use it. Get the sound of voices into your story. Have characters say things that record their style of speaking, or have them say something that reveals their nature:

> When we got safely down the hill, we sat in the pine needles listening to the whack of tennis balls and the voices of the players making line calls.
>
> "Bobby, what if the bear attacked"?
>
> I looked down at Mark who was staring up at me, still some fear in his pale green eyes.
>
> "I'd have picked you up and run down the hill faster than lightening. Don't worry, I'da got us out of there. You trust me, don't you, kid?"
>
> "I trust you, Bobby."

6-4 Planning Your Narrative

The beginning of this chapter presented a simple sequence for a narrative essay: background, episode, commentary. When creating background, you generally go from broad background to more focused background, until you are describing the setting and circumstances in which the episode will take place.

When you compose the episode, imagine you are writing a script for a television soap opera or situation comedy. Those programs open with a scene of some kind, with characters standing around talking or doing things. Then the screen goes black for an instant and when we return we may be somewhere else, perhaps with a new mix of characters, who are sitting around talking or doing things. Then the screen goes black again. . . . The series of scenes add up to the episode.

You can block out those scenes into an outline before writing. Plan background and commentary into the outline as well. Here's a sample outline for a narrative essay:

Background:
—Broad background: tennis tournament summers
—Broad background: enjoyment of the woods with my brother
—Focused background: Description of setting, the forest hillside where the episode will take place

Episode:
—Scene: me climbing hill and finding bear
—Scene: me running down hill, can't find Mark, see him, go to him.
—Scene: we escape

Commentary:
—what I learned
—how it has affected my life ever since

Don't feel obligated to rigidly follow any plan that you create. Planning is a good way to get started on an essay. However, it shouldn't interfere with your work once you get going. Suppose, for example, you started with the outline above, and then as you were writing one of the scenes you felt a need to stop and make a comment on what was happening. Do so, even though the outline shows commentary coming only at the end. Do what feels right as you are composing. What feels right doesn't turn out well every time, but you can always revise later. Often you can't know if something will work until you put it down on paper and try it out. Your broad plan should keep you generally on course, so a few deviations won't hurt.

7

The Informative Article

Some essays are written mainly to inform. They report on research, or they transfer knowledge and expertise. During college, you will probably learn how to do scholarly research reports in your major area of study. That kind of writing is highly technical in nature and has to be learned in courses within the specific discipline. A research report in biology, for example, must be learned in the context of doing biological research.

Another type of informative article simply educates general readers about a subject. And still another kind helps readers perform a task. Both of those are common assignments in composition courses, and both are discussed in detail below.

Informative writing generally operates on either of two levels of sophistication, according to your "audience," your expected readers. As the writer, you are an "expert" in the subject. The levels of sophistication are

- Expert-to-expert
- Expert-to-novice.

Expert-to-expert is the kind of writing you learn within your major. In a composition course, you will most likely write expert-to-novice informative essays. In most cases, you can assume that you are writing for the "general educated public." Or, to put it another way, you are writing for your fellow students and your instructor. These readers are intelligent and can figure things out, but they know less about your subject than you do. Compared to you, they are novices.

When writing informative texts, you have to worry about novice readers being able to understand what you are saying. It is very important to keep your audience in mind as you plan, draft, revise, and edit. So we will begin by taking a close look at audience analysis.

7-1 Analyzing an Audience

As you plan the first draft of your informative essay, ask yourself:

—What do I want my readers to know about this subject?
—What do my readers already know? What will I have to tell them?

In other words, plan your essay not on the basis of the subject itself, but on the basis of your purpose and your audience's initial level of knowledge.

Your purpose might be to provide your readers with a general sense of something, such as the complexities of rigging (setting up) a sailboat for sailing. Or you may wish to give your readers a complete, detailed set of steps for accomplishing the rigging of a certain kind of boat. These different purposes would lead you to provide different kinds of information. In the first case, as you looked at how sailboats are generally rigged, you might provide concrete detail to show the complexity of one aspect of rigging of a particular kind of boat, just as an example. In the latter case, you would have to provide such detail for each step, and you wouldn't be interested in communicating general principles of rigging.

As for your readers' initial state of knowledge, their possible lack of familiarity with the technical vocabulary of the subject is an obvious concern. You might assume that a general educated audience will know the meaning of terms like *bow, stern,* and *mast,* but not terms like *sheet, jib,* and *halyard.*

However, what about terms like *boom* and *tiller*? Will you have to define either of those? That's the kind of question that competent writers carefully consider.

If writing an educational essay, you might use a neutral tone, but in giving instructions, you might use a friendly tone to ease any fears the reader may have about the complexity of the task. That's the psychology behind those slaphappy "Dummy" books you see everywhere.

Any large audience may include members with very different levels of initial knowledge. Technical writers talk about writing for a "reasonable person standard" or an "ignorant person standard." Which approach they choose would depend on their analysis of their audience and their purpose in writing. So here's another question you need to ask yourself as you write your essay: Do you need to write for the least knowledgeable or least proficient? Or just for the average reader? The answer to that question can depend on whether it is necessary that *everyone* understand *everything*. If you are trying to give a general impression of what rigging a sailboat is like, the answer is probably no, not everyone has to understand everything. If you are trying to explain to senior citizens how to vote using a new ballot design, the answer is undoubtedly yes, everyone has to understand everything.

When you analyze your audience, consider not only the readers' purpose in reading and their level of knowledge of the subject, but also their demographic characteristics: age, gender, educational level, or ethnic/racial/regional identity. You normally wouldn't write for middle-aged businessmen the same way you would write for teenaged girls.

The readers' predisposition toward the subject can also become important. Are they enthusiastic to learn about this subject? If so, that makes your task easier. Or do they see the learning task as a necessary evil? If so, you may have to emphasize its importance. Is what you are writing essential to your audience? Or are your readers free to toss your text aside and read or do something else? If the latter, then you will have to capture their attention and hold it.

7-2 Writing to Educate

In the context of a composition course, writing to educate means providing an overview of a topic for the purpose of enlightening your audience. The model essay in Box 5-1, entitled "A Beginner's Guide to Investment," provides an example of this kind of writing (see p. 72).

Finding a Subject to Write On

In searching for a topic for this kind of article, explore your own areas of expertise by looking in these places:

—your employment background
—work you have done around the house
—volunteer work
—unusual experiences (climbing a mountain, digging for clams, dealing with an injury or illness)
—sports you have played or otherwise know a lot about
—hobbies (baseball card collecting, cooking)
—personal intellectual interests you have pursued on your own (history, poetry, theatre)
—subjects you have studied in school
—experiences at school (preparing for the SAT, working on the yearbook).

You may have an interest in a subject, but not a great deal of initial knowledge about it. For example, you may have wondered how tough Marine boot camp really is. Or how the Supreme Court decides whether or not to hear a case. If the assignment schedule gives you enough time, you can build up your expertise through research.

A Writing Process

Here is a straightforward writing process for creating a first draft of an informative essay:

1. Select a topic you know about or are interested in learning about.

2. Do a purpose/audience analysis: what do you want to accomplish; what does your audience initially know and not know? Will you write for an average or least knowledgeable audience? Will you have to allay fears or distrust? Will you have to arouse interest in your subject, or will it be inherently interesting to your audience?
3. Brainstorm and do research for ideas that will serve as the main areas you will cover; you might write these down in the form of section headings for the report.
4. Decide what order to present the sections.
5. Select an easy section to start with and begin drafting that part; continue until all sections are written.

The Introduction

Some writers delay writing the introduction to their informative essay until after they have written the large middle section, the "body." They find it easier and more logical to introduce a discussion if they know what the discussion will include. But sooner or later, you will need to write that first paragraph or two that leads your reader into your main discussion.

Your beginning should clearly establish the topic and leave the reader with a sense of the direction of the essay. Very formal academic essays often directly state what subjects will be covered. *English Journal,* an academic publication for high school and college English teachers, publishes instructions for writers which include this description of the required beginning:

> The introductory paragraph of the article should clearly indicate the direction of the manuscript. Overly discursive or vague openings are not appropriate for the readership of *English Journal.* Beginning paragraphs should clearly indicate: what the manuscript addresses; why anyone should care to read it; and why the writer is qualified to speak on the subject.

In other words, the *English Journal* editors want you to state:

> —the topic
> —its importance
> —the basis of your authority.

Obviously, you are not restricted to that kind of opening in a composition course, but an *English Journal* beginning may work well, depending on your topic. For example:

> Working on weekends with my father, I have helped to construct more than 50 garages. In some of these projects, we have made at least minor errors in measurement. In a few cases, we have had to tear down and rebuild a section. Those errors were costly. In this article, I'm going to identify the different places where measurement errors occur and show you how to avoid such errors when you go to build your own garage.

You may need to attract the reader's attention. As in the paragraph above, you can do that by pointing out the importance of the subject (such as avoiding costly construction errors). You can also grab attention with a dramatic statement of opinion or fact, an interesting quotation, a startling statistic, or an anecdote (a very brief story that illustrates a point). The example below starts with a quotation that makes a dramatic statement, and then relates it to the reader:

> "Almost one in five women will be, in some manner, sexually assaulted before they graduate from college," according to the National Center for the Protection of Women. If you are a female student at Pumpkinville College, you could be one of those victims. If you are a male student, you could end up accused of assault or harassment.

Another standard way to begin an informational essay is to define a key word. Let's say your title is "Ending Date

Rape." You might begin by defining the key term *date rape*. In an extended definition, this may involve quoting policy statements from one or more of your college's official publications and from other sources you have examined (to become an expert). You might want to create a few scenarios—dating scenes in which date rape occurs—to clarify the concept.

In the above case, you would be writing a long beginning to fully describe the problem, in preparation for your solution. Chapter 8 provides a detailed presentation of the problem-solution structure for essays.

The Body

The nature of the subject itself, its natural parts and structure, will affect what you say about the subject. But you probably won't say everything you know or could say. Your purpose and your audience's needs should be the guide to selecting information to present. If your topic is date rape, what do your women readers need to know? What do your men readers need to know? What are you trying to accomplish in this essay—are you trying to convince students that a problem exists? Or are you trying to convince the reader to accept a particular definition of date rape? Or are you trying to reduce the incidence of date rape at your school? Answering such questions will help you decide on content.

How should you present the information in the body of your essay? Besides the methods of development discussed in Chapter 3, you can also use drawings and other illustrations to clarify points you make in your text. See the discussion of "visuals" in the section below on writing instructions.

As for the order in which information will be presented, your first consideration should be to present necessary background information, if later understanding will depend on it. That's why starting with an extended definition of a key term is a common approach.

The following are typical strategies writers use to make decisions about the order of presentation:

—chronological (ordered by time: first this happens, then this . . . etc.)

—easiest to understand to most difficult to understand

—familiar to unfamiliar

—shortest (quickly covered) to longest (requires more development)

—most interesting or important to least interesting or important (because readers will stop reading the text if they get bored early)

—visual (close up to far away; far away to close up; around the outside; inside to out; outside to in; left to right or right to left; high to low or low to high).

The Conclusion

Your informative essay really ends when the body ends. At that point you have passed on the information you wanted your reader to have. Nevertheless, you should add at least one final, concluding paragraph to close down your piece of writing. Below are some of the things writers do in conclusions. You can do more than one.

- Restate the importance of the subject.
- Restate the main point, now not as something you will prove, but as the logical conclusion from what you've said about the topic (e.g., Judging by the experience of Pumpkinville College, it seems clear that the best way to reduce the occurrence of date rape is by educating both men and women on what constitutes date rape and the circumstances that lead to it).
- Mention other texts (books or magazines or Web resources) the reader might consult for more information on the topic.
- Indicate what remains unknown about the subject and where further research needs to be done.
- Make a prediction about the future based on what you have written (e.g., Within our lifetime, we will probably see the end of the internal combustion engine in automobiles).

- Give a warning (e.g., Never be casual about taking measurements during a construction job. As we have seen, the consequences of even the slightest error can be disastrous).

- Make a hopeful statement (e.g., The major problems of dentistry have been solved. We know what people need to do to care for their teeth. As dentists get better at communicating that information to their patients, we can expect more and more people to retain all of their teeth for all of their life).

- Call for action (e.g., Parents of school children in every community should insist, loudly, that their schools do not give up their full, rich curriculum for the limited focus of test-preparation drills).

The conclusion is not the right place to introduce new ideas about your topic that the reader would expect you to develop.

Box 5-1 provided an example of an informative paper that relied heavily on quoted sources. Box 7-1 shows an example of an educational essay written from general knowledge.

Box 7-1 An Essay that Educates

<table>
<tr>
<td>The title and beginning stimulate reader interest in what otherwise might be seen as a dull subject</td>
<td>

The Secret Killer

Are you too heavy around the waist? Do you know someone who is? Are any of your older relatives living a sedentary couch life? All such people are candidates for developing "adult-onset" diabetes, now simply called Type II diabetes because so many children and young people are being diagnosed with it. It's also called "the secret killer" because, if undetected, it can lead to loss of limb, blindness, or death. A third to a half the people with Type II aren't aware that they have the disease.

</td>
</tr>
<tr>
<td>Development through extended definition, using contrast</td>
<td>

In Type I diabetes, the body doesn't produce insulin, which is used to transfer energy (sugar, or "glucose") into muscle and other body cells. The person with Type I must take insulin shots. In the case of Type II diabetes, the body converts foods into insulin in a normal way, but the body cells resist taking in the glucose. The insulin isn't working, and the person's body is said to be "insulin resistant."

</td>
</tr>
</table>

continued

Box 7-1 An Essay that Educates *continued*

Since the topic is a medical condition, the writer develops the essay by describing causes and treatment

For Type II diabetics, insulin resistance results mainly from carrying too much fat above the waist and from consuming too many carbohydrates (pasta, beans, rice, potatoes, bread), which don't yield their glucose easily. Too much glucose in the blood over time destroys the body's organs. Treatments involve weight reduction and changing one's diet to reduce the intake of fatty foods and carbohydrates. Daily exercise is also a part of the treatment, because that requires energy, which means that the muscles pull more glucose from the blood. Exercise also burns fat and reduces weight. Many people with Type II diabetes also take medicines that overcome the resistance.

The essay ends with friendly advice

The next time you get a physical, have your blood checked for diabetes. The best prevention is to live a healthy life: eat modest portions of good foods (including carbohydrates) and exercise regularly.

7-3 Reveal Your Organization

We have talked about using simple outlines in the planning stage of writing. Those outlines reveal the organization of the essay to *you*, the writer. You should also reveal your organization to your reader as the essay progresses. This is particularly true in the case of informative articles.

Sometimes, as the writer of an informative article, you might tell the reader in the introduction what the essay will cover, in what order. But even if you do that, you should continue throughout the essay to orient the reader by indicating what has been discussed so far and what is coming up next. For example:

Now that we have seen some of the bad consequences of sloppy measurement during the foundation stage of building a garage, let's look at what happens when a builder makes inaccurate measurements in the carpentry work.

The first part of that sentence looks backward to what has just been discussed, while the second part looks forward to what is coming up next. The author of the model essay in Box 5-1 uses this sentence to indicate a major shift in the direction of her discussion:

> Once you have decided to invest your extra money, you must decide whether to invest in stocks and bonds.

That sentence tells the reader that the focus on whether or not to invest or save is over, and the essay will now look at investment options.

During your final editing session, look for places where these "sign post" or "transitional" sentences would be helpful to the reader, and plug them in.

7-4 Writing to Instruct

Creating a set of instructions is a popular composition assignment. It appeals to teachers as "real world" writing, since your instructions can be put to use on campus or elsewhere. To do this writing well, you need a good sense of audience. In most cases, you should be writing for the "least proficient" user, and your instructions should be "idiot proof."

Title

Begin with an informative title, such as:

—Using the Photocopier in Henderson Library
—How to Log On to the Campus Computer Network
—Daily Animal Care in the Zoology Lab
—Designing a Personal Fitness Program

Preliminary Information

Before you begin your instructions, provide necessary preliminary or background information. For example:

> You cannot log on to the campus network unless you have a university account.

If you are explaining how to do something that requires tools or ingredients, list those tools or ingredients in the preliminary section. For example, one dentist's handout on homecare after deep cleaning begins like this:

> Follow the instructions below for the next 3 days. If your mouth feels sensitive after 3 days, continue this routine for 2 more days. You will need:

> ~an Endtuft brush
> ~Peridex
> ~Colgate Total or other suitable toothpaste, such as Regular Crest or Colgate with fluoride
> ~Prevident 5000+
> ~a Perio-aid (toothpick holder with toothpick).

Visuals

Short instructions often employ visuals in the form of line drawings, shaded drawings, or photographs. The visuals support the text and illustrate the steps. If your instructor says nothing about visuals, and you think they might be helpful, ask if you can use them. Box 7-2 shows how visuals can be used to make actions clearer.

Box 7-3 shows two different types of labeling, the first using "call outs" and the second using a "legend."

Warnings

Instructions sometimes require warnings, to prevent missteps that could have seriously bad consequences. The warning should always come *before* the step that may lead to trouble.

Professional technical writers often put a warning sign in the left margin. The conventional warning sign is an exclamation point inside a triangle. Then, at the beginning of the

Box 7-2 Use of Visuals with Instructions

How to Tie a Bowline Knot

Pronounced "bow-lin," the bowline knot is used to create a secure loop, such as you would find at the end of a ship's painter, the line used to secure the bow to the dock.

1. Form a small loop, curving the line over the top of itself.

2. Create a large loop (a) and then pass the end of the line up through the small loop (b), then around under the line (c), then down through the small loop again (d).

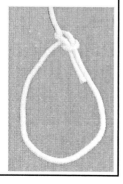

3. Pull the end of the rope tight, securing the knot.

Box 7-3 Different Methods of Labeling a Visual

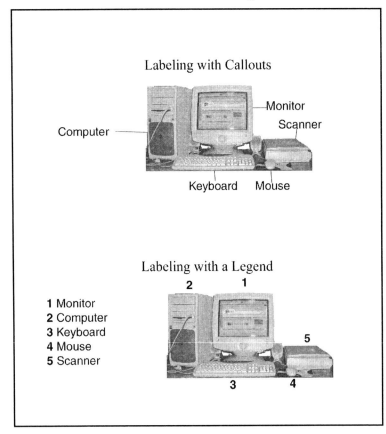

first line of the text next to the warning sign, they put an appropriate warning term, according to the seriousness of possible trouble. The American National Standards Institute (ANSI) has proposed these trouble levels and these warning terms:

>**DANGER!** (serious physical harm *will* occur if the warning is ignored)
>**WARNING!** (serious physical harm *may* occur if the warning is ignored)

CAUTION! (minor injury may occur if the warning is ignored)

NOTICE! (the product or machine may be harmed if the warning is ignored)

IMPORTANT! (your own work may be damaged or set back if the warning is ignored).

Warnings should be noticeable. You don't want your reader skipping over them. The warning statement itself would typically indicate:

1. what the danger is
2. what the bad consequences may be
3. how to avoid the problem.

For example:

In the next step, you will save your document using SAVE AS.

IMPORTANT! Be sure to use SAVE AS, not SAVE, or you will overwrite your original file. When you perform this action, hold down the mouse button firmly until SAVE AS is highlighted. Then, and only then, release the button.

STEP 4: Save using SAVE AS. Give your file a new name.

Steps

Always number steps.

If the number of steps starts to get large, let's say eight or more, then break them up into sections, perhaps three main actions with several steps to accomplish each action. Box 7-4 shows how this is done.

You may simply want to tell the reader what to do in each step. Or, you may want to provide more elaborate information, such as what each step does, what to do, what to expect if things go right, and what to do if things go wrong. If providing this kind of extensive information, consider using a table format as in Box 7-5. Check with your instructor to make sure that a table format will be acceptable for this assignment.

Box 7-4 Model Instructions with Two Levels of Steps

Rigging a Hobie 16 Beach Catamaran

These instructions tell you how to prepare your Hobie 16 for sailing.

Step 1 Remove the boat from your trailer.
1) Back up the trailer close to the water.
2) Undo all straps and tie downs.
3) Unhook the winch line.
4) Roll the boat carefully off the back of the trailer.
5) Slide the boat around so that it faces the wind.

Step 2 Step the mast.
Stepping the mast means raising it to a vertical position.

Important! While the mast is being raised to a vertical position, its base should be held in position by a pin apparatus. Do not try to step the mast without that pin in.

---

1) Attach the side stays.
2) Set the base of the mast in the well and insert the pin.
3) Step onto the trampoline, and, starting from the back, lift the mast and walk forward, raising the mast as you go.
4) Undo the pin.
5) Attach the forestay.

[The directions would continue in this manner.]

Box 7-5 Using a Table Format for Instructions

How to Make Tasty Scrambled Eggs for Two

Advance preparation: Chop 1/4 cup each of onions and mushrooms. Chop 3 cloves garlic. Chop 1/8th cup each of fresh basil and parsley. Beat four eggs in a bowl and add salt and pepper to taste. Measure a tablespoon of olive oil.

	TASK	DO THIS	WHAT TO LOOK FOR
Step 1	Prepare pan	Heat pan and add olive oil; drop one piece of chopped onion in the oil	Onion will sizzle audibly if the pan is ready
Step 2	Cook onion, garlic, and mushroom	Toss ingredients in the pan and move around with spatula	Onions become trans-transparent; mushrooms dark
Step 3	Cook eggs	Add beaten eggs to pan; move around with spatula	Eggs mix with other ingredients, slowly firm and approach desired consistency
Step 4	Spice up the eggs	Add basil and parsley; give eggs a final scramble	Herbs are evenly distributed

Plate immediately.

Usability Testing

Do a quick test of your instructions by carrying them out yourself. Then make any necessary changes.

Finally, perform a "usability test," in which you watch a member of your intended audience perform the task following your instructions. Observe closely and take notes on any hesitations or mistakes. Ask the user to name any points of confusion. If the user makes a mistake, stop the process and get it back on track so that the usability test can continue.

Revise on the basis of the test.

8

The Argument on a Controversial Issue

The word *argument*, here, doesn't mean shouting and shaking fists at one another. It refers to the educated, civil, reasoned debates that editorialists and scholars engage in. These writers try to persuade the reader to accept, or at least respect, their viewpoint. Many composition courses nowadays focus partly, if not exclusively, on argumentation.

Most types of writing include some element of persuasion. Even a mode like description can require persuasion. If you believe that a particular piece of fruit is appetizing, then your goal in describing that fruit is to convince the reader that your judgment, your taste, is correct. Literary interpretations require persuasion. If you assert that one lesson we should draw from the tragedy of Shakespeare's *Romeo and Juliet* is the futility of romance, then your job in writing that essay is to persuade the reader to agree with you, or at least understand and respect your opinion.

However, argumentation constitutes a slightly different form of persuasive writing from those others. With the argumentation essay, you are addressing a controversial issue or idea, usually well known to the public or to a clique of experts, and you are using certain established, formal methods of presenting your case.

We will start by looking at "classical argumentation," the kind in which you take sides on an issue and try to convince your reader to agree with you. A more contemporary form of argument seeks compromises, and we will look at that also.

8-1 The Three Appeals

In his book *Rhetoric*, written over 2,400 years ago, the Greek philosopher Aristotle pointed out three broad categories on which argumentation can be based: authority, emotions, and logic.

The Appeal to Authority

You can persuade your listeners or readers by appealing to their respect for expertise, experience, and integrity. You do that by referring to what well-known, honored authorities have said on the subject. When introducing a person you are quoting, you can also indicate that person's credentials:

```
Robin Williams, the author of best-selling books on
print design, warns us that "if two elements are sort of
different, but not really, then you don't have contrast,
you have conflict" (53).
```

Or you can point out your own qualifications to speak on the issue at hand; in other words, you can tell your reader why your opinion has a high value:

```
I spent six years in the Army, so I know what it's like
to have your life planned for you every day. That's what
I saw the scout leaders doing at the camp.
```

The Appeal to Emotions

Emotional appeals are sometimes dismissed as corrupt, particularly when the writer seems to be trying to horrify the reader into forming an opinion without thinking deeply. You can imagine this happening in the debate over abortion. Those who oppose abortion might vividly describe an aborted fetus as looking human-like. Those who support a woman's right to an abortion might describe a young girl sitting in her bathtub with a coat hanger. These gruesome images create a revulsion towards one view or the other, but neither presents a line of reasoning that can be evaluated.

Nevertheless, respected intellectuals do make appeals to emotion. A stirring anecdote recounting the regret the writer's sister feels years later about having had an abortion in her youth is a legitimate use of example. Regret is an emotion, but it obviously has a place in this discussion. The sorrow created in the reader's mind from such a story is an emotion, but one that seems logically justified. Another writer might just as legitimately arouse anger in the reader by recounting the violent harassment that some doctors have experienced for performing legal abortions. It is reasonable to become angry at those who use violence against people they disagree with.

When your main goal is to arouse strong emotions, you are making an appeal that your instructor might criticize. However, there is nothing wrong with making a sound argument that happens to arouse emotions.

The Appeal to Logic

Finally, you can appeal to your reader's rational mind through logic. There are many different approaches under this category, including the methods of development already discussed in this book, such as *example*. The existence of an example of X constitutes a logical reason for believing in X. If I say that you should reject abortion as an option because you may later regret it, my argument will be enhanced by my recounting how that happened to my sister. The example proves that such regret is a real possibility.

Comparison also constitutes a way of reasoning about your subject. On the abortion issue, people taking different sides would focus on the similarities or the differences between a fetus and a baby. *Cause* and *effect* is another branch of reasoning. Certain causes tend to produce certain effects. When the economy improves, crime drops. One way to fight crime, then, would be to fight poverty. A frequent line of reasoning used in arguments is an appeal to *history*. If something has happened in the past, it is reasonable to assume it could happen today. If before abortion became legal, many young

girls killed themselves trying to perform abortions on themselves, then it is logical to assume that if abortion becomes
illegal again, many young girls will suffer that fate again.

You cannot expect to convince all your readers by force
of logic alone. Human logic is a flexible device, not a rigid
road to truth. In the abortion debate, for example, one can
make a logical case for seeing the fetus as fully human and
one can make a logical case for seeing it as less than human.
For some people, one logic will be stronger than the other,
and they will take their stand on that basis. But many others will
choose one logic over another because they want a reason to
oppose abortion or to support it, because doing so fits in with
their broader set of beliefs and concerns.

With an argumentation essay, you cannot expect to win
over the hearts of all your readers. However, you can present
your case so that all readers see the logic behind it.

your goal is only to present your case

8-2 A Basic Argument Structure

The approach to argumentation presented in this section may be all you will need for your composition course.
Here is a workable outline for an argument essay:

Include your

1. Description of the topic and controversy *Tell what the issue*
2. Summary of your opponent's view *Know the other side of it*
3. Concession to that view
4. Rebuttal of that view
5. Your view and its defense.

It isn't necessary to treat the above structure as a new
kind of pre-structured essay. Think of the five elements listed
there as options, things you can do when creating this kind of
essay. The order above is a natural one, but don't hesitate to
create your own order. For example, as you present your
opponent's view, you may wish to respond to it point by
point, instead of waiting until the view has been completely
presented in a block. Or you may wish to begin with a brief

look at your view on the subject, and then turn to the views of others who disagree with you.

Let's look at each element of this simple but effective approach to argumentation.

Statement of the Topic and Controversy

A good way to begin your essay is by establishing:

1. what the controversial issue is, and why it is controversial if that is not obvious
2. your position, what side you are taking.

Below is a beginning for an argumentation essay that does those two things. By the end of the paragraph, you know what the issue is and what side the writer is on.

> In her senior year of high school, my sister discovered to her horror that she was pregnant. She and her boy friend had broken up months earlier, and he was now engaged to another woman. Afraid that the pregnancy would ruin her life, my sister got an abortion. But it didn't really solve her problem, because she immediately regretted denying that child a chance to live. She replaced a manageable problem, pregnancy, with one that will never leave her, a life-long sadness and regret. This is just one reason for opposing abortion.

Summary of Your Opponent's View

At some point, the author of the above essay would want to begin presenting the opposing view, perhaps with a sentence like this:

> Those who support abortion argue that it's a privacy issue, that a woman has a right to control what happens to her own body.

Here are some phrases you can use to introduce the views of others:

—Those who support X argue that. . . .
—Those who oppose X point out that. . . .

—Those who argue that X. . . .
—Those who defend the view that X. . . .
—Opponents of X often point out that. . . .
—Advocates of X say that. . . .
—Those who advocate X believe that. . . .

We have looked at methods of summarizing in Chapter 5. Within the context of argumentation, it is important that your summary of your opponent's view is fair and complete. An unfair, "straw-man" presentation, in which an extreme, distorted version of the opposing argument is presented for easy ridicule, will probably be recognizable as such, even if your readers are not familiar with the viewpoint being summarized. If they are familiar with it, they will definitely conclude that you are untrustworthy.

You must recognize and present at least the strongest of your opponents' arguments. If you are responding to a single published essay, you should, first of all, talk about the arguments in that essay as if some of your readers have not read the text; that is, you need to present the lines of reasoning in full for their benefit. However, you should simultaneously assume that some of your readers are intimately familiar with the text and know every argument the writer makes. If you leave out an important argument, those readers may conclude that your opponent has won the debate on the basis of that neglected argument, which you haven't been able to answer.

You may be arguing against not just one author but a whole category of people: "those who believe X." For example, those who oppose additional gun control laws, or those who favor more restrictive gun laws. In that case, you must again present the strongest arguments of your opponents. To do that, you have to become familiar with the public debate. As you read articles on both sides of the issue in preparation for writing, make a dual-column list of the main points and supportive lines of reasoning that show up in the essays. In one column put the view you support, and in the other column the opposing view. These notes can then be consulted as you compose your first draft.

3) *Concession*

I can see this is true, but the fact still remains that . . .

Concession means admitting that your opponents are correct. It isn't likely that your opponents in an argument are totally wrong. They must have some rational reason for believing what they do. When you disagree with a person or a group, you usually disagree with only part of what they believe. Clarify where you stand by acknowledging points of agreement. At the same time, you will enhance your own credibility as a fair-minded person by making concessions.

Here's an example. The first sentence is a concession.

> It's true that some women who have an abortion later deeply regret it. However, most don't, and we have to balance that occasional regret with the tragedy of bringing large numbers of unwanted children into the world.

Notice that the writer doesn't waste any time turning away from the concession toward making an argument in support of his/her own position. You don't want to make the other view seem attractive by dwelling on the ways it is correct. Make the concession quickly, and then turn to your view. Signal that turning point by using a pivot word like *however.*

Below are seven types of concession, with a sample "turn away" for each. When searching for a point to concede, you can agree on the following:

1. Your opponents are correct to believe that the issue under discussion is important or that action is required (but perhaps wrong about the solution): McCarthy is correct when he says that fighting poverty in Islamic countries is a key part of fighting terrorism. However, his approach to fighting poverty there would be ineffective.

2. Your opponents are ~~correct that the problem~~ is real (but perhaps ~~wrong in thinking it is important~~): I don't disagree with Jones when he points out that some teachers are incompetent. However, most aren't, and a much greater problem is the need to recruit new teachers.

3. Your opponents are ~~correct about certain facts~~ (but perhaps ~~wrong about others~~): Jackson correctly puts the state debt at 11 million, but he is wrong when he suggests that most of that debt had been accrued before the new administration took office.

4. Your opponents are ~~correct in their description~~ of an occurrence (but perhaps ~~wrong in their interpretation of~~ its meaning): It is true that the boy who opened fire on fellow students at McCoy Central School was carrying several guns which he had recently purchased through the mail, but that doesn't mean that stronger gun control laws would have prevented this tragedy.

5. Your opponents are ~~correct about the cause of a problem~~ (but, again, perhaps ~~wrong about its solution~~): I agree that poor communication in this organization results in people acting on misinformation, but flooding employees with daily notices and weekly flyers is not the best way to solve the problem.

6. Your opponents are ~~correct about the solution~~ to a problem (but perhaps ~~wrong about the implementation~~ of that solution): Without doubt the Florida Fish and Wildlife Conservation Commission should use volunteers to help develop paddling trails in the Apalachicola River swamp, but it should not sponsor expeditions by inexperienced volunteers in mid-May when the alligators are most active.

Some phrases for initiating concessions:
- *admittedly*
- *granted*

- *to be sure*
- *certainly*
- *I agree that*
- *there's no doubt that*
- *undoubtedly,*
- *I concede that*
- *Smith is correct when he says that*
- *Smith has a point when he says that*
- *of course*
- *naturally*
- *no one disagrees with the contention that*
- *it is true that*

Some pivot expressions for turning away from the concession toward the response:

- *but*
- *however*
- *yet*
- *on the other hand*
- *nevertheless*
- *despite*
- *although*
- *even though*

4 Rebuttal

Rebuttal means showing what's wrong with an opposing view. Never present a view you disagree with without rebutting it. Don't leave any of your opponents' points hanging there unanswered.

Suppose you feel strongly that your opponent's reasoning is somehow wrong. How can you discover and expose the weakness in that reasoning? Below are eight possible weaknesses in your opponents' arguments that you can look for:

1. Your opponent's argument may be based on a false premise (a premise is an unspoken assumption):

Smith says that "There are many reasons for the failure of our public schools." But his assumption that schools are failing may be wrong. Two decades of rising test scores suggest that our schools are better than ever.

2. <u>Your opponent may be making factually incorrect statements</u>:

Smith says that our school children do not compare well on international comparisons. It is true that American kids have compared poorly when average Americans were put in competition with elite students in other countries. However, Berliner and Biddle show that when those comparisons are done reasonably and professionally, American children perform very well.

3. <u>Your opponent may be making a "false analogy" (an inappropriate comparison)</u>:

Smith argues that schools are less efficient than successful businesses. But schools should not be compared to businesses. They are not out to make a profit; they are out to serve the public. They can't behave like companies and "sell off" or "close down" weak segments of the student body. They have to teach everyone.

4. <u>Your opponent may be exaggerating or over-generalizing</u>:

Smith says that "Many graduates of public schools cannot read." Actually, when someone graduates who cannot read, it is so unusual that the story makes the national news.

5. <u>Your opponent may underestimate the importance of something</u>:

Smith dismisses the importance of money, saying that school achievement can't be bought. Admittedly, money isn't everything, but it does matter. Recently in Texas, poor children began performing much better after the state provided money to improve teaching materials.

6. <u>Your opponent's logic may contain a self-contradiction or inconsistency</u>:

Smith calls for "leaving no children behind"; yet his voucher approach to helping children in impoverished schools leaves 90% of them behind in those schools.

7. <u>Your opponent's solution may not work</u>:

Smith wants to impose massive standardized testing as a means of raising standards. However, test preparation curriculums don't raise standards in the sense of increasing learning. They dumb down the syllabus to the study of testable items.

8. <u>Your opponent's solution may work, but may create new problems</u>:

To encourage science majors to enter the secondary teaching profession, Smith wants to pay science teachers more than history and English teachers. This will undoubtedly result in more science teachers, but it will discourage good English and history majors from going into teaching, and it will create serious antagonisms among existing faculties in America's schools.

Those are just some of the possibilities. In general, look for places where your opponent's reasoning depends on incorrect information or derives from a misunderstanding of the situation. Also consider the implications of what your opponents are saying. People often overlook or ignore some of the undesirable effects of the policies or actions that they propose.

Presenting and Defending Your Own View

In presenting your view, apply the advice in Chapter 3 about full development. ~~Don't just state your position on the issue—teach it.~~ *Justify what you've said.*

In the course of fully presenting your viewpoint, you should anticipate any objections to your reasoning that may arise in your readers' minds. If those objections are left unanswered, your whole argument is weakened. Here a writer anticipates and then responds to an objection:

> The federal government can help address the inequities of financing that leave some schools inadequately funded. Those who are concerned about maintaining "local control" of schools need not be. Federal assistance can be managed without sacrificing local control. Richard Rothstein, the education columnist for the *New York Times*, has outlined an approach in which the federal government gives money to states, so that states can distribute it to impoverished school districts to be used at the local schools' discretion.

In that example, the writer anticipates that certain readers will object to a solution that would decrease local control of schools.

When planning and writing your argumentation essay, you don't have to give equal emphasis to attacking your opponent's arguments and presenting your own view. You can give extra weight to one or the other, though you would normally want to do both to some extent.

Box 8-1 provides a sample essay that follows the argument structure described in this section. The emphasis in this essay is on rebuttal, showing how the opponent is wrong.

8-3 A Problem-Solution Structure

The problem-solution structure assumes that the topic can be visualized as a problem that needs to be solved. An outline might look like this:

Box 8-1 An Argument Essay

Fixing Our Schools: A Response to Smith

Identification of the issue and summary of the opponent's views. The writer's position is implied.

Jasper Smith, in his essay "Let's Fix Our Schools," decries what he sees as the decline of our public school system. He argues that many American kids graduate without being able to read their diplomas. He points to international comparisons which show our students performing worse than kids in impoverished third world countries. Smith's solution is to create a system of vouchers that will allow students in poor performing schools to escape to high performing suburban schools or to private schools. Smith also wants to find ways to break up teacher unions and fire incompetent teachers.

Concession

Rebuttal: attacking the opponent's presentation of the facts.

It is true that some students have graduated from American public schools without being able to read. However, those cases are so rare that they make the national news. As for international competitions, the idea that an impoverished third-world country has a better school system than ours is not believable. In fact, most children in the country Smith mentions don't go to high school, and many who participated in the comparison tests were American children of military or diplomatic personnel, or natives attending elite private schools, often run by Americans (Markus 89-90).

Rebuttal: attacking the opponent's false premise.

Backing up the point with information; teaching the subject.

We don't have a proficiency problem in this country. As Shirman points out:

High performers headed for Ivy League colleges, who scored an average of 1000 on the original SAT in 1941, now score between 1200 and 1400. In the past fifty years, the percentage of young people graduating from high school

continued

Box 8-1 An Argument Essay *continued*

has risen from about 50% to 85%, and in the past two decades the percentage of those attending college has increased by 40%. These students have entered college with stronger backgrounds in core and science courses than any group in the past, and a higher percentage of them have graduated from college. (71)

Rebuttal: attacking the opponent's solution.

Smith's voucher program doesn't solve anything, since it leaves most kids behind in underfunded schools with too few trained teachers using outdated textbooks and broken down science equipment. The way to solve the problems of weak schools is to fund them adequately. According to educational columnist Richard Rothstein, we can do this without giving up local control by giving federal grants to poor states to disperse among their poorest schools.

Concession

As for incompetent teachers, granted they exist, but a more important problem is finding the thousands of new teachers we will need in the coming decades. Our teachers are an aging group and mass retirements are coming soon. Again, the federal government can help out with state grants, and state and local governments can encourage good students to go into teaching by raising salaries. Many college students take money into account when choosing careers. For example, a student undecided between nursing and teaching might make the choice on the basis of present salaries in those professions.

The Writer's View of the Problem

The writer's solution.

Why the solution will work.

We can all help by ending the unjust public criticism of our teachers, which drives good teachers out of the profession, while discouraging young people from taking it up.

Ends with another solution and an appeal for action.

1. Statement of a problem
2. False solutions that have been proposed or tried out, or that the reader might think of
3. Why those solutions won't work
4. Your solution
5. Why your solution will work.

In some cases, the reader's interest can be taken for granted; in others, not. If the reader's interest is not obvious, you might begin by showing readers that the problem is theirs, not just someone else's. That's a decision you have to make as you analyze your audience (for a discussion of audience analysis, see Chapter 7). Here's a beginning in which the writer points out the relevance of the problem to the reader:

> About 88 percent of our youth now finish high school. However, in some areas among some groups, the high school non-completion rate runs as high as 60 percent. That may not seem important to you, especially if you are not a member of one of those groups or you do not have school-aged children, but, in fact, that high drop out rate affects everyone. The days when someone could drop out of school and immediately find employment in a local factory are gone. Young people without a high school diploma have little chance of finding a decent job, and many turn to crime. The rest of us become their potential victims, until they get caught and we have to pay for their incarceration with our tax dollars.

In some instances, the definition of the problem may constitute the main controversy. For example, are weak public schools, where they exist, the result of under-funding, poor teaching, or a bad curriculum? In each of those cases, certain solutions are obvious, once the problem has been determined. If under-funding is the problem, then more funding will solve it; if poor teaching is the problem, then better teacher training is called for; if the curriculum is bad, then it must be changed. So, in a short essay of this type, the problem itself would be the main focus, and the solution might be handled briefly. Instead of false solutions, you would talk about misunderstandings of the problem, and why they are misunderstandings. Box 8-2 provides an outline for an essay focusing heavily on the nature of the problem. It does look at a solution, but only quickly at the end of the essay.

Box 8-2 Outline for a Problem-Solution Essay: Heavy Focus on the Problem

---

Thesis: High schools do indeed lack an intellectual atmosphere, but not, as James Conant says, because of an overemphasis on sports.

Misunderstandings of the problem:

1. Conant says that sports distract students from school work
   —only the tiny percentage who play are distracted from their studies
2. Conant says that the community encourages an obsession with sports through its attendance at games and other activities.
   —raising school spirit through community involvement in sports has no effect on what goes on in the classrooms; sports are weekend activities

The Real Problem

1. Classroom presentations are boring
   —Too much lecture and test
2. Students aren't interested because they don't do their home-work
   —If you learn about a subject, it starts to become interesting; students never get into the subjects

Solutions

1. More projects and less lecture
2. Parents need to insist that their children do their home-work;
   —Teachers should send assignments to parents

In other cases, everyone may agree on the problem, but different groups offer different solutions. If writing on the drug problem in the U.S., for example, you could do so by looking mainly at the different solutions that have been proposed, saying little about the problem itself. Other topics call for a more balanced discussion of problem and solution. How much emphasis to put on the different parts of an argument is an important choice you must make as a writer.

8-4 A Compromise Argument

Another characteristic of the problem-solution design is that it opens the door for a compromise approach to argumentation. Instead of trying to convince the reader to embrace one side or the other, you look for common ground and seek a solution acceptable to many people on both sides of the issue. This is good practical training since, in democracies, many social issues end up being solved politically through compromise. Box 8-3 illustrates a beginning and ending for a compromise essay.

Box 8-3 Beginning and Ending for a Compromise Argument

Many politicians and journalists have harshly criticized our public schools in recent years. They have described our school system as a "failure," and have claimed that the quality of education our schools offer has declined. Others, mainly educationists, have taken the opposite view. They point to a variety of statistical evidence to support their claim that our public schools are better than ever and that we don't have a proficiency problem in this country. Both sides in this debate have something to offer as we try to improve our schools.

[The body of this essay would supply details of two arguments.]

continued

Box 8-3 Beginning and Ending for a Compromise Argument
      continued

> Those concerned about proficiency must admit that, regardless of how much failure we can find in our public schools, there is a lot of success out there, too. We have no problem, for example, supplying our Ivy League schools and best technical universities with highly qualified students ready for the challenges of the most demanding curriculums. Whatever failure exists is not national, but exists in certain schools and among certain demographic groups. Likewise, those who argue that we don't have a national problem of proficiency must admit that the general success of our public schools does not extend into every corner. For example, most schools may have graduation rates of more than 90%, but some groups in some states have completion rates below 50%.
>
> Instead of devising national solutions which only mess with the success of most schools, and instead of ignoring the problems of some schools because schools in general are doing a good job, let's focus our attention on those groups of students and those schools which do have real proficiency and drop-out problems. We should be able to bring to bear an array of solutions, applied locally, not nationally, once we understand that the problems are real, but not universal.

To figure out a compromise solution, look at the issue from the perspective of one group and then the other. What does each side really, ultimately want—institutional improvement, peace, fairness, redress of past wrongs, respect, authority? Often they both want the same thing, the same outcome. And often the way to get there is through a recognition of the legitimate concerns of each side, as well as a sense of what each side will have to give up. Let's pretend we are UN peace negotiators for a moment and try to imagine how we could bring about a peace between the Israelis and the Palestinians— no easy task!

What do the Israelis want? Let's assume that most of all they want a recognized, secure nation in peace. What about the Palestinians? The same. For Israel to get what it wants it has to give the Palestinians what they want, and visa versa. For Israel to give the Palestinians what they want it has to accept the idea of an independent Palestinian state and it must give up its building projects in Palestinian territory. For the Palestinians to give the Israelis what they want, it has to withdraw its demand for the return of millions of Arabs to Israel and return of their property (that would ruin Israel) and it has to clamp down on internal groups that would threaten the security of Israel with terrorist attacks.

A separate compromise might have to be fashioned to address the governing of Jerusalem. What do both sides want in that city? Go on from there.

Out of those ideas you could fashion an argumentation essay that built the outlines of a compromise solution to the Palestinian-Israeli conflict. A compromise argument is more sophisticated than a classical argument. It is a challenging approach, and if done reasonably well, your instructor will probably be impressed.

However, if the assignment calls for you to take sides on an issue, and you'd like to submit a compromise solution instead, ask your instructor if that would be OK. **Never vary from an assignment without getting permission first.** Your instructor may have definite reasons for wanting you to follow instructions exactly as they have been given.

9

The Literary Criticism Essay

Literary criticism doesn't mean saying bad things about a piece of literature. Instead, *criticism* in this context means (1) interpreting the meaning of a poem, short story, novel, or play, (2) explaining how that piece of literature creates its effects, and (3) evaluating the work. In a composition course, you will probably not be expected to make judgments about the quality of a literary work, but you may be asked to do the first two tasks, interpretation and analysis of method.

A professional critic will read and write about a piece of literature differently than you will, because the professional knows all of the author's works, knows where the author fits into the broad history of literature, knows how the author imitates his or her contemporaries, knows how the author is unique among contemporaries, and knows what creative writers have done and what they generally do with various genres (novel, short story, poem, or play).

You probably know none of that.

Nevertheless, your composition instructor may ask you to write an essay in response to a poem, a play, or a piece of fiction. This chapter shows you how to compose an interesting essay about a piece of literature, despite your lack of background in literary studies.

9-1 Personal Meaning and Community Meaning

Your education, perhaps, has taught you that a poem or a piece of fiction has a single "meaning," which expert readers can figure out and you can't. Your job as a literary critic is to discover and reveal that correct meaning, which of course you can't do. However, don't despair. Advances in psycholinguistics and reading theory have rendered that "one meaning" view of literature untenable.

Scholars looking into the nature of reading have made an interesting discovery: No two people can possibly read the same complex text, such as a piece of literature, precisely the same way. Reading ultimately consists of creating a text in your mind through contact with a written work. However, the particular mental text that you create will be strongly affected by conditions outside the written text, the three most important being (1) your purpose in reading, (2) your culture and era, and (3) your prior personal experience with the subject matter of the written text.

As for purpose, experimenters have found, for example, that people remember different details after reading a description of a house if they are told to do so as potential home buyers or professional thieves. The two groups of readers create different texts in their heads.

How you read a text depends on who you are culturally: your nationality and ethnicity, as well as the effects of the times that you live in on your view of the world. People living in 17th century New England would read a story about witchcraft differently than people living in Nebraska today.

As for personal experience, suppose we are reading a paragraph which says that a cat suddenly appears around the side of a couch and walks across the room, and that paragraph provides no details about the cat. Everyone brings different experiences with cats to such a reading. Some of us might see a white cat moving gracefully, others a gray cat moving stealthily, and others an orange cat hopping playfully. Yet we are all reading the same text.

But that's not the whole story. Most of us read the cat passage in very similar ways, as well. We all have about the same sense of what a cat is. We imagine a house cat, not a bobcat or a tiger. The word *couch* evokes in our minds similar images. And what happened in the scene was the same for all of us. We read the passage alike, quite simply, because we belong to the same culture in the same era.

So for each of us, the text has both a unique "individual meaning" and a shared "community meaning," to use terminology developed by the literary theorist Stanley Fish.

This duality of meaning allows for two approaches to literary criticism. In one approach, you discuss what the text means to you, how it connects to your personal experience. In the other, you talk about what the text means to a community, to all human beings or to all members of some group, like Americans or Mexican Americans or Southern women.

Your instructor may require, or allow, either of those two approaches—the pursuit of personal or community meaning. As part of understanding your assignment, make sure you know what is allowed and what is required.

9-2   What is Meaning?

We've been talking about the meaning of a piece of literature as if it were obvious what "meaning" means in regard to a poem or a play or a story. But in fact, that's not obvious at all, even though it is what you want to get at, to write about, when you write either of the two papers mentioned above.

Given this kind of assignment, it is best not to worry about the piece of literature as having meaning of its own, but instead to think in terms of what meaning you can bring to the literature. In other words, the important questions are:

—how is the text meaningful to *you*, personally?
—what broad community meaning can *you* see in the text?

This makes you the active meaning maker, instead of the text. And that's what you have to do when you write this kind of literary criticism: Make meaning.

A good way to start creating the meaning of a literary text is to use the personal approach. You can later extend your personal reaction to a community meaning, if that's what your instructor wants in the final version of the essay. Here are some things that may be meaningful to you personally, as you read a literary text:

- **The pleasure the language affords you**, your enjoyment of the interesting or attractive sounds coming from the text, your delight in the beautiful phrasing. In poetry especially, the sound of a poem can affect your mood or contribute to some of the effect. Always read a poem aloud a couple of times, as well as silently.
- **Your reaction to the narrator.** If the poem or story has a narrator, a fictional person speaking the poem or telling the story, listen for the tone of that person's voice and consider how that speaker strikes you—is the speaker a delicate lady, a cool dude, a con man? Do you like or dislike the narrator as a person? Do you trust what the narrator says? Who does the narrator remind you of in your personal life?
- **The evocation of a memory** of some event that was important in your life, perhaps an event that shaped who you are, or made you realize something. Now you are being reminded of the event in circumstances that allow you to reconsider it.
- **The recognition of yourself** being described, providing a clearer understanding of who you are.
- **The recognition of a type of familiar person** being described, deepening your understanding of that person, or type of person, perhaps someone important to you such as a parent or friend, or a type of person you know from your circle of friends, such as a daredevil or an ambitious person.
- **The recognition of a place**, or type of place, which is a part of your life, perhaps evoking a set of memories. Such descriptions renew and sharpen your sense of

this place—why is it important to you? What details in the piece of literature bring back the memory?

- **The recognition of a smell**—autumn leaves burning, the heavy heat of a locker room, your mother's perfume—so that you relive an episode or a time in your life, regaining those memories. This may lead to a comparison of then and now. Not only smell but other senses—visual images, the feel or taste of something—can stir up memories and ideas.
- **The evocation of a feeling:** a sense of regret that you once felt, or the elation over some accomplishment, or the nervous ecstasy of love, suddenly coming over you as though you were going through that experience again—what do you know now that you didn't know then?
- **The recognition of a story line**, of how human character leads you, or others you know, on a familiar course to a foreseeable end; an understanding of why things happened as they did in your life.

And then the extension of these evocations to the community:

- **The recognition of not just yourself and individuals you know, but of a community**, such as Catholic high school students, Bronx residents, the oystermen of the Florida panhandle, the elderly living their last months in an institution. Or even the recognition of your country as a community, perhaps a sense of national destiny.
- **A recognition of our humanity, our similarity with others**, and from that a new understanding of what it means to be human.
- **Our place in the universe**, perhaps alone and insignificant, perhaps integrated and important.

Box 9-1 provides a short poem by the respected poet Robert Francis, and Boxes 9-2 and 9-3 provide two short interpretations of the poem, a personal interpretation and a community interpretation. Take a moment to read those boxes before going on to the next section.

Box 9-1 Robert Francis's "The Hound"

From *Robert Francis: Collected Poems*, 1936-1976 (Amherst: University of Massachusetts Press, 1976, copyright © 1976 by Robert Francis). Reprinted with permission.

The Hound

Life the hound
Equivocal
Comes at a bound
Either to rend me
Or to befriend me.
I cannot tell
The hound's intent
Till he has sprung
At my bare hand
With teeth or tongue.
Meanwhile I stand
And wait the event.

Box 9-2 A Personal Interpretation of "The Hound"

Francis's "The Hound"
by Steve Student

1 In his poem "The Hound," Robert Francis uses a dog
2 approaching at a run to represent uncertainty in life. For
3 me, this is an apt image. When I was a kid about twelve, I
4 used to roam the middle class neighborhoods of my hometown,
5 and there was one street that I always walked with fear. In
6 the middle of the block, the residents of a fine brick home
7 sometimes allowed their boxer to run free. This was not a
8 sweet animal. If I were walking by on the street, it would
9 growl and race toward me. I'd "stand and wait the event."

continued

Box 9-2 A Personal Interpretation of "The Hound" *continued*

10   Although the dog seemed to always stop at the edge of
11 the yard, ten feet from me, I would creep away slowly and
12 fearfully, listening to its growls, worried that it would
13 suddenly attack. As an adult, I am still sensibly afraid of
14 an unknown dog that comes running at me, but there are
15 differences. For one thing, now I would avoid that street.
16 I'm more willing to take a longer route to avoid risks. As
17 a result, life is not as threatening as it used to be. I
18 don't see the hound so often. Also, I am not as afraid of
19 the hound as I used to be. I know my odds against any thing
20 that threatens me. I can stand up to a dog, if I have to.
21 When I was a kid, angry dogs just frightened me.
22   "The Hound" evokes in me old fears, but it also makes me
23 realize that those were childhood fears, from a time when I
24 didn't understand much about the world, when the future was
25 as "equivocal" as the approaching hound. I am more knowl-
26 edgeable now, and therefore stronger.

Box 9-3 A Community Interpretation

Francis's "The Hound"
by Sally Student

In his poem "The Hound," Robert Francis uses a dog approaching at a run to represent uncertainty in life. Will the dog lick me or bite me? Will I live a good life, or a tormented one? This is a reasonable question, since we can look around us and see people who have everything, including happiness and a long life, and we can see people who have nothing, who are miserable and die young.

According to Francis, we cannot know what our fate will be: "I cannot tell / The hound's intent / Till he has sprung / At my bare hand / With teeth or tongue." We are in the dark. And this is true to some extent. A person's fate can change at any moment. Today you are rich and happy, tomorrow the stock market crashes or someone slips on your front steps and you are sued and end up in debt and miserable. Or one day a lover abandons you and you are miserable; but in the end you find someone else who is much better for you. We cannot predict what will happen to us.

continued

Box 9-3 A Community Interpretation *continued*

```
     Yet I am unsatisfied with this poem. It doesn't tell the
whole story. The poem's narrator is too passive: "Meanwhile
I stand / And wait the event." He is too vulnerable: the
hound leaps "At my bare hand." Aren't there things that we
can do to take control of our own lives? Can't we learn from
experience? For example, a woman who has had only abusive
relationships with men recently, as she begins to get in-
volved again with a new man, must feel like the narrator
watching the approaching hound. But she doesn't have to
passively wait to see what happens. She can seek men who are
not likely to be abusive. She can test the men she goes out
with. She can make it clear to these men what she will not
put up with. She need not "stand and wait the event."
```

9-3 Writing an Essay on Personal or Community Meaning

Try following the steps below for writing an essay on personal or community meaning. Let's assume that you are
working with a short text, such as a poem or short story.

A Seven Step Writing Process

1. Read the poem or story once, allowing yourself to
   enjoy it without worrying about anything else—
   except vocabulary. Put a check mark next to any
   words you don't know the meaning of. If reading a
   poem, you can do that on the second reading.

2. Look up the words you marked in a dictionary and
   write definitions in the margin of the text. If you are
   using a borrowed text, photocopy it and mark up the
   copy. In fact, working with a photocopy is a good
   strategy even if you own the text, because a copy is
   more portable and it affords more room for marginal
   comments and even back-of-the-page ruminations.
   (A small personal photocopier is a handy device to
   own for college work in general.)

3. Reread the text, looking for personal connections, and, if you are writing a community interpretation, also any community connections or "lessons" that you might notice. When a thought occurs to you, put a note in the margin immediately.

4. Start your essay by introducing the text by title and author (Robert Frances, in his poem "The Hound," creates a situation in which . . .). Box 5-2 on page 76 shows variations on this kind of sentence.

5. Spend a paragraph or two summarizing the plot, introducing the main characters, or explaining the author's main point. That's what Sally does in her first two paragraphs (see Box 9-3). It's important, however, that you don't devote most of your paper to plot summary. That's a common mistake. Assume that the reader has read the piece of literature and already knows what happens. It's not the plot itself, but what you see in it that matters. Any extensive discussion of the plot should be related to what it reveals about the characters and perhaps about yourself.

6. Begin to develop your idea, your personal connection or the community meaning. You might create a question, and then begin to answer it. Or you might begin with a statement of how the piece of literature connects to your life.

7. As you develop your ideas, continually refer to the text, occasionally quoting. This is crucial! You must demonstrate that the ideas you are advancing can reasonably be derived from the text. You do that in two ways: (1) connect your writing to the text by using the text's vocabulary and talking about its themes (big ideas), as Steve does in Box 9-2, and (2) point to and quote relevant passages in the text as evidence that what you are saying is connected to the text, as Sally does in Box 9-3.

How Steve and Sally Connect the Reader to the Text

Steve makes references and connections to the text in these lines: 9 (a quote); 14 ("unknown dog that comes running at me"—an image from the text); 18 ("the hound"—which here has become a symbol of anything threatening); 22 (a reference to the title); 25 (a key word quoted: "equivocal"); and 25 ("approaching hound").

One out of four lines in Steve's essay has a direct connection to the text. Even though Steve is talking about himself, he keeps his reader continually in touch with the poem. With the personal-meaning essay, you may have a tendency to stray from the literary work too much, so concentrate on making many connections through vocabulary and images.

Note that Sally also connects you to the text quite often, and she does more extensive quoting to prove her points. With the community-meaning essay, since you are not just reporting on your own mind, you have a larger obligation to prove the reasonableness of your ideas. So when writing that kind of essay, you need to quote and refer to passages in the text that support your reasoning.

Use the Present Tense

When you are describing the actions of characters or what an author does when writing a poem or piece of prose, **use the present tense**. Write "the hound races toward the narrator," not "the hound raced toward the narrator." Write "Francis has his narrator stand passively instead of resisting," not "Francis had his narrator stand passively instead of resisting."

9-4 Literature as Art

When writing an essay of the kind described above, it is useful to say that you bring meaning to the text. But it is also true that the author had some intention while writing. Even though authors are not to be trusted entirely when they talk about their own work, and even though artistic texts tend to take on a "life of their own" as the authors work on them, we know that authors' intentions show up to an important extent in creative writings. We know this because we can see a particular consistent view of the world in many works by the same author. For example, it is unlikely to be coincidence that one author consistently portrays human characters as victims of their circumstances, while another consistently creates heroes who rise above their circumstances to triumph against all odds.

So you, the reader, are not the only meaning maker.

When professional critics write about literature as art, they try to show the methods by which the author or the work creates meaning. When talking about meaning in this sense, we can use the term "theme." Literary works have "themes"; that is, they develop major ideas, some of which are quite standard and reappear in many works: loss of innocence, loss of faith, maturation, corruption of society, good versus evil, the ugliness of war, the beauty of love, the meaninglessness of life, the necessity of freedom, the interdependence of people. Note that these themes may contradict one another. Different writers view the world differently.

If you were to write an essay about a piece of literature as a work of art, you might trace how the setting, or certain images, or the symbols the author has created contribute to the development of the themes of the work. To do so in depth requires a substantial introduction to literary criticism, including some technical terminology. Some colleges do offer a first-year course which combines composition and the study of literature, but most don't.

Much more likely in a composition class, when your instructor wants you to write about literature as art, the instructor will ask you to do a character study. A character study is an essay which shows how the author connects a fictional character's nature to the outcome of the story. You won't need a background in literary criticism to do a character study, but you will need to study the text closely.

9-5 The Character Study

Thousands of years ago, the Greek philosopher Heraclitus intoned that "A man's character is his fate." In other words, the kind of person you are determines what happens to you in life. Works of fiction are carefully written to illustrate that principle. When doing a character study, your job is to show how a fictional character's background and personal attributes determine the character's behavior and lead to the outcome of the story, or at least the outcome for that individual.

Along with Heraclitus's principle of character, you should be aware of the generally accepted idea that all stories involve a conflict. A fictional character fights against

—himself/herself (internal conflict because of the person's dual nature or dual desires)
—the natural world (such as the sea in a storm)
—God or some other element of the supernatural
—another character in the story
—a group (such as the local community, which may disapprove of the person)
—humanity (Moliere's *Le Misanthrope* is a play about a man disappointed with the corrupt nature of people).

The outcome of the story is the resolution of that conflict. *Resolution* means that the final stage in the conflict is reached, at least for the characters; the conflict may or may not be over. Some conflicts never end.

Your instructor may give very general assignments when asking for a character study, so as to give you a lot of freedom to do what you want with the assignment. Here is a typical character-study assignment of that type:

Choose a character from one of the two short stories we read and write an analysis of this person.

You might flourish under that freedom. However, some students work better when given more direction, as in this assignment:

> Choose a character from one of the two short stories we read and write an analysis of this person. Describe the person's background, personality, and relationship to other characters. What crucial role does this character play in the story? How does this person's character determine his/her actions? How do the person's actions determine, or contribute to, the outcome?

If you get the first assignment, you can always write it as if you had been given the second.

Here are four starting points, any one of which you might find useful:

1. Simply state that a character is a particular kind of person: Jack Jones is an incurable romantic or Sarah Smithers represents pure evil. Then prove your assertion by showing how those characteristics emerge from the descriptions, dialogues, and plot. Then show how the character trait affects the outcome of the story for the character.

2. Look for a contradiction in the person you are writing about, and use that as the starting point for your paper. For example, in Salinger's *The Catcher in the Rye*, the main character, Holden Caufield, is both cynical and kind. Ask yourself: In what directions do these contradictory characteristics pull the person?

3. Look for a question you can raise about the character:

> Why does George feel that he has to kill his friend Lennie at the conclusion of Steinbecks's *Of Mice and Men*? Not everyone would do that. What is it about George's character that makes him choose this solution?

There's your first paragraph, leading to a thesis question. You would answer the question through your analysis of the character, backing up what you say with references to the text.

4. Look for a conflict in the plot: the person you're writing about in conflict with the bad side of his/her own personality, or with nature, or with God, or with another person, or with a group, or with humanity. Ask yourself: How does the character of the person determine the outcome of that conflict?

The model paper in Box 9-4 shows how the loss of innocence in the main character leads to conflict and a particular kind of resolution.

Box 9-4 A Character Study

The Outsider

Krebs, the protagonist in Hemingway's "Soldier's Home," has lost his innocence fighting in Europe in World War I, but he has gained a certain integrity from having been a good soldier. Now he is back in his hometown in Kansas, and he can't fit in. He has changed, but "Nothing was changed in the town" (112). Because of his loss of innocence and new integrity, he is in conflict with his family and his community.

To start with, he came home late, a year or so after the war was over and all the "hysteria" and hero worship was long finished. When he tried to talk about his experiences, he found that no one was interested; everyone was jaded with exaggerations and lies. When he tried briefly to fit in by lying, it only made him sick: "Krebs acquired the nausea in regard to experience that is the result of untruth or exaggeration" (112). The lying almost ruined the war experience for him, an experience that had been very important to him. It soiled his integrity. It was a harsh lesson and it put him off from trying to fit in.

Krebs admires the pretty girls that parade past his front porch, where he sits reading a history of the war. He is attracted to them, but, we are told:

---

continued

Box 9-4 A Character Study *continued*

He did not want to get into the intrigue and the politics. He did not want to have to do any courting. He did not want to tell any more lies. It wasn't worth it. (113)

He preferred his relationship with the women of war-ravaged France and Germany: "It was simple and you were friends" (113). The world of the small Kansas town is too complicated, in silly ways. As for the girls, "the world they lived in was not the world he was in" (113).

Krebs finds himself in conflict with his mother, who can't understand who he has become. She wants him to get a job and settle down, become a responsible citizen. Fit in. Become "a credit to the community" (115). Krebs will have none of that. She says, "God has some work for every one to do. . . . There can be no idle hands in His Kingdom." Krebs replies, "I'm not in His Kingdom." The scene is embarrassing and awful for both characters. In the end, to make his mother feel better, he tells her he wants her to pray for him. In other words, he has to lie again.

As a result of this scene, Krebs realizes that he can't stay in his "soldier's home," or even in the community. It won't work. He can't fit in. So he decides to clear out:

He had tried to keep his life from being complicated. Still, none of it had touched him. He had felt sorry for his mother and she had made him lie. He would go to Kansas City and get a job and she would feel all right about it. (116)

Like many Americans who left small towns for foreign lands and the trauma of war, Krebs can never be the same again. He has to find a new way to live, even a new place to start out. Krebs apparently hopes that in the anonymity and sophistication of a big city he may find the uncomplicated peace that he wants.

Work Cited

Hemingway, Ernest. "Soldier's Home." *The Complete Short Stories of Ernest Hemingway, The Finca Vigia Edition.* New York: Charles Scribner's Sons, 1987. 111-16.

10

The Long Research Paper

The research paper assignment requires you to learn about a subject through library and Internet research, and then write an informative report on it or a lengthy argument. Your instructor will likely spend a great deal of class time teaching you methods of research, particularly the use of resources available in a college library and a method of note taking. You can also look forward to a detailed coverage of MLA parenthetical note form and Works Cited formats (Chapter 5 in this book should prepare you for that).

This chapter provides an overview of the whole project and offers some advice on carrying it out that you may not get from your other learning sources. Before beginning such a project, however, it is important to understand the concept of plagiarism, which is the presentation of someone else's phrasing or unique ideas or research results as if that phrasing or those ideas or those results were your creation. One of the challenges of writing a long research-based paper is making sure that you continually give credit where credit is due, continually distinguishing between your own thinking and expression and original research and that of others. Chapter 5, which talks about bringing in outside sources, should be helpful.

Here is generally what you have to do to write the first draft of a research paper:

1. Find a good topic.
2. Create a tentative organizational plan.
3. Create a working bibliography.

4. Become an expert and develop a set of notes.
5. Write up each section.
6. Edit for plagiarism.
7. Create the Works Cited.

Let's look at each of those activities in detail.

10-1 Find a Good Topic

Your instructor will probably limit what you can write about. You may have to choose a literary topic, for example. Or you may have to take sides on a controversial issue. Probably the easiest assignment is to provide an informative report on some subject, such as the irregularities in Florida balloting that led to confusion during the Bush-Gore contest. We'll develop that topic as an example in this chapter.

You want to come up with a topic that has these characteristics:

1. **It interests you.** Or it holds potential interest. If you are interested in politics in general, then the Florida balloting topic would almost certainly become interesting as you got into it. If political issues bore you, then this might not be a good topic. The research paper is a long project, so you don't want to make it utterly brain deadening by choosing a topic you can't get interested in.

2. **It's not too broad.** Trying to write on all the election irregularities that occur in U.S. elections would be too large a subject. You want to work with a subject that is narrow enough that you can cover the whole topic.

3. **It's not too narrow.** On the other hand, you're going to have to write eight to twelve pages (or even more) on your subject, so don't choose a topic so narrow that you can't write that much about it. You might be

hard pressed, for example, to spend eight pages talking about the voting irregularities in Palm Beach County.

4. **Information is available.** The Florida balloting topic will become a better and better subject as more books and articles come out. About six months after the 2000 election, the first books were emerging; there were a lot of magazine and newspaper stories available; one anthology of essays had come out on the legal ramifications; and law journal articles abounded on the involvement of the courts. Right after the election, there probably wasn't enough information available, but six months later there was.

10-2 Create a Tentative Organizational Plan

This step is crucial. The sooner you can focus your research on the various sections that your paper will include, the less time you'll waste on unproductive reading. As soon as possible in the process, write down what you think might be the subtitles for sections of your paper. For example, for the Florida election paper, you might imagine these:

I.   problems with ballot design
II. inconsistencies in how counting was done
III. conflicts between the state government (run by Republican Governor Jeb Bush, George W. Bush's brother) and the state supreme court (largely Democratic appointees)
IV. the Supreme Court's controversial involvement.

Notice that the sections are numbered with Roman numerals. That allows you to label notes easily. Any note discussing the Supreme Court, for example, would have a IV in the margin. Later you'll put all the IV's together when you go to write that section.

If you don't know enough about your topic at the outset to make educated guesses about subsections, make those guesses as soon as possible once you start reading. These subtopics become the categories into which you put information as you come across it. The sooner you have the categories, the sooner you will be able to evaluate a source as to whether or not it is relevant to your paper. If it fits into a category, then it is something you should consider reading. If it doesn't, you ignore it.

10-3 Create a Working Bibliography

You find out whether or not there is enough information available by creating a working bibliography, which is a list of possible sources. Many articles, books, and news stories in your working bibliography will eventually be used, but many will not be, and some you may not even look at, once you have sufficient information to write the paper. So a working bibliography is not a Works Cited. The Works Cited will consist of those sources you actually used and referred to ("cited") in your text.

The working bibliography does two things: It tells you whether there is sufficient information available, and it provides you with a reading list that you can use to become an expert and, through note-taking, to compile information. It also provides you with hints about how the subject can be broken up into sections.

Here's a step-by-step process for creating a working bibliography:

1. **Learn the library.** Most college libraries print maps showing what is on each floor and in each room, as well as handouts showing how the library computer system works. Ask a librarian for these materials. Pay attention to what your instructor says about library and Internet resources in general. Your instructor

may have your class take a tour of the library. If so, don't miss class on that day. If you do, arrange to join another class taking the tour. The tour will help you find out what kinds of books, reference books, documents on film, journals, and magazines are available in your library and where they are located. The tour will also help you learn how the electronic indexes in your college library work. Those are the computer files showing what's in the library. They will be your main searching tool.

2. **Dig up possible sources.** Using the computer indexes and other tools you have learned about, gather the titles and locations of as many books, articles, Internet texts, and news stories that you can find that relate well to your topic. One of the best techniques for finding good sources is to take your best sources so far and look at their bibliographies. That will tell you about earlier works written on that subject. A "citation index" will tell you about texts that cite your best articles, providing more recent publications on the subject. Ask a librarian to help you find citation indexes. Librarians, as a group, are nice people who enjoy helping students. Don't be reluctant to ask for their help whenever you need it.

3. **Evaluate available sources.** If you can't find much, consider broadening your topic or changing it altogether. If you come up with an overwhelming number of relevant books and articles, look around for a subtopic within that bounty, and make that your new topic. In other words, narrow your topic down to something manageable. If you are required to use about ten sources for the actual paper, create a list of the best fifteen to twenty that you can find.

4. **Photocopy.** Photocopy articles and chapters and the title pages of books you may use from your school

library. Take down any information you will need for a bibliography (see Chapter 5).

5. **Submit requests for interlibrary loans** for articles and books you are interested in but which are not in your library.

6. **Type your list in MLA format.** Put your 15-20 potential sources in MLA format for a Works Cited. Such an effort guarantees that you have the necessary information about each source, it familiarizes you with the sources you have found, it teaches you how to do Works Cited formats, and it gets most of the Works Cited work out of the way. Creating MLA entries is unexciting grunt work. Nobody is going to make it fun for you, so accept it for what it is and simply do it. With practice, it'll become quicker and easier. As you work on your paper, you may discover new sources that you want to use. Add them immediately to the working bibliography.

10-4 Become an Expert and Develop a Set of Notes

You become an expert first through background reading, then focused reading. For background, you read the most general or all-inclusive text(s) in your working bibliography, such as an article in a reference book or a whole book on your topic. Next, you look at book chapters and articles that focus in on different aspects of your subject, namely those aspects you intend to write about. And which aspects are those? Look to your tentative organizational plan. Or start developing one.

To repeat: You need those categories, those subtopics, in order to know what to read and what not to. And later, you will use those subtopics to organize your notes and your whole paper.

By the time you go to write your ten-page paper, you should be able to write a five-page paper off the top of your head, without looking at any notes, but just by recalling what you know about each aspect of your topic. That's what it means to become an expert.

Once you start reading, especially focused reading, begin to take notes. The notes are your reminders of what you can say about your subject when you go to write about it. Your instructor or your English handbook may show you a method for note-taking that employs 3 X 5 cards. There's nothing wrong with that, though there's nothing wrong with using whole sheets of paper, either. Just make sure that you label each note with a Roman numeral to indicate which section of your paper it belongs to.

Instead of using notecards or blank pages for notes, you can photocopy pages from your sources, then mark passages and write your own thoughts in the margin. Of course, you'd put a Roman numeral in the margin to categorize the marked passage and your comment. One advantage of this approach is that you know what statements are yours (the marginal notes) and what statements come from the source (the photocopied passages). There's never any confusion leading to plagiarism.

Regardless of what method you use, as you take notes, you must do three things

1. **Keep track of sources.** Note which bibliographical entry (which text) in your working bibliography the note is taken from—and what page(s) it comes from in that text! In some cases you will need the page numbers for your in-text parenthetical note; in all cases, the page numbers will be useful if you have to return to and re-consult your original source. If the source is new and isn't yet in your working bibliography, be sure to add it to the bibliography immediately, before you forget to do so. If you lose that information, or don't take it down in full, you cannot

quote from that note in your paper or draw any unique information from it. One of the most frustrating things that can happen to you as a researcher is to have in your notes an important piece of information or a wonderful quotation, but not be able to use it because you've lost track of where you got it from.

2. **Categorize each note.** Forgive the repetition of this point, but this is important. Let's say that your paper will have four parts to it, four sections. Using Roman numerals, number the sections according to what order you think you will use for the organization of your paper. Then put one or more of those Roman numerals next to each note. You can put down more than one number because a note may be relevant to more than one section, and at this point you don't know where you are going to use it. So write something like II & IV, and when you go to write section II, check out this note, and when you go to write section IV, check it out. You might photocopy the note and put one copy in the II pile and one in the IV pile. (Again, an inexpensive photocopier is a great tool for college work.)

3. **Clearly distinguish quoted material.** When you eventually go to use a note, perhaps a month after taking it down, you will need to know whether or not the note is your own thought, or a summary in your own words of someone else's thinking, or the exact words of an author you are borrowing from. Create a system of labeling, if that will help: MT (my thought), SUM, Q. Some students use two different color inks, one for quoted phrases and sentences and one for phrases and sentences written in their own words. Do whatever you can to remain highly conscious of this crucial distinction between your own thinking and

wording and that of your sources. Doing this at the note-writing stage is an important first step in avoiding plagiarism.

10-5 Write Up Each Section

You might begin by working first on the section that will be easiest to write. That will get you warmed up for the rest of the text.

You have two possible approaches to producing the first draft from your notes. The conventional way is to put your notes in a stack in the order in which you want to present the information and ideas in them. Then you write from your notes. Working this way, however, you run the risk of producing a text which bounces from one idea to another without creating a coherent whole. As you write, you're seeing only trees and not the forest.

You might try another approach. Read over your notes and then put them away where you can't see them. Then write the section as you would any other essay, from memory of the facts and understanding of the issues, but also with a sense of what you want to communicate to the reader. This puts more of you into the text. Of the many voices that contribute to your paper, your voice should be the dominant one.

When you've done what you can to create a short draft of this section of your paper working from memory and understanding, take your notes and go back to your text and fill in information you forgot and put in quotations where they would be effective. Writing first without your notes in front of you also makes it easier to avoid plagiarism. When you bring in your notes, you can always add in-text, parenthetical notes to indicate that published authorities agree with you about some point or that the point is someone else's original idea.

If this second approach doesn't work for you, go back to the traditional method of writing directly from your notes.

After the first draft is complete, read over your paper to see how it comes off. You may find that a portion of one section doesn't seem related to the rest of the section and doesn't really contribute anything. Cut it. You may find yourself entertaining questions about your topic that your paper raised but didn't answer. Do more research and expand that part of your paper. You can continue to do research and fiddle with sections right up to the last moment.

10-6 Edit for Plagiarism

Besides the normal editing you would do to smooth out awkward phrasing and correct errors, you should do a final edit for plagiarism—the "theft," or unacknowledged borrowing, of ideas, data, or phrasing. English instructors usually take plagiarism very seriously. Some actually spend hours in the library tracking down evidence that a student copied a passage into his or her paper. They may also use computer search programs that find passages on the Internet as a means of catching electronic theft. Most colleges have policies that result in an F in the course in cases of serious plagiarism.

Plagiarism occurs at the content level and the phrasing level. As you read over your paper, ask yourself about each major point: Where did I get this idea? If it is your own conclusion or interpretation of the facts, fine. If it is a point made by more than one writer you encountered, fine. That means it is information "in the public domain," and you don't have to cite your source. But if you got the idea from one other source only, it may be unique to that source, so add a parenthetical note to give credit to that author.

It is easy to allow well-written expressions from other texts to seep into your notes and from there into your paper without quotation marks around them. As you read, ask yourself: Could I have written that sentence? Is that my language? Do I normally use that word? If the answer is no, it's still possible that your involvement in the topic has led to an increase in vocabulary and a familiarity with phrases used by many who write on this topic. Fine and good. But it may also mean that you have simply copied someone else's words into your text without quotation marks around them. Check it out.

10-7 Create the Works Cited

Now that you know which works you have actually cited in your paper, it is time to do the final bibliography, the Works Cited. First, determine which sources have parenthetical notes and make sure that they are listed in the Works Cited. Use the search function of your word processing program to find the parenthesis punctuation mark to locate each note. Check off each note in your working bibliography and create the Works Cited from the checked entries. That way you can make sure that *only works actually cited* end up in the final Works Cited and that *all works that have been cited* end up there.

Here are the three major mistakes writers make in terms of form:

1. **Misspelling the names of people and publishing companies.** Your spell checker won't help you here. Do a separate proofread for this.
2. **Putting an entry out of alphabetical order.** Proofread for this by looking at each entry and the one just below it to see if the bottom one belongs earlier. It only takes half a minute.
3. **Wrong punctuation.** Do a separate proofread for this. Have models of correct form handy, perhaps checked off in your textbook as you created the original entries in your working bibliography. All Works Cited entries end with a period. Check down your list for that final period.

10-8 Decide Not to Cheat

Outright cheating on a research paper takes several forms: deliberate massive plagiarism, copying a paper whole from the Internet, having a friend write the paper, getting a paper from a fraternity or sorority file, or buying a paper from an agency that sells them as "research tools." While minor plagiarism may get you a reduced grade or an *F* on the paper, cheating can get you kicked out of school.

Many composition instructors nowadays are involved with their students during the writing process; that is, they are examining notes and early drafts. That approach nips plagiarism in the bud and makes cheating more difficult than doing the work honestly. Nevertheless, some students cheat on this assignment, often because they remain hopelessly confused about how to write such a paper or because they get behind and run out of time.

Instructors usually know when a student has cheated, because the writing is noticeably superior to what the student has been producing in the course. English teachers are very adept at analyzing and evaluating language. Even a slightly improved phrasing and analytical ability jumps out at them. Knowing, of course, is not the same as proving. Some instructors put in a lot of time searching for evidence of cheating. They usually find it. Others don't bother. They shrug and chalk you off as "just another loser." If the instructor wants to press the issue, even without evidence, you may be called into the dean's office to produce your notes and to prove that you are an expert in the subject you supposedly researched and wrote about.

There are alternatives to cheating. If you are confused, and your research isn't going well, you can ask for a meeting with your instructor in his/her office. Your instructor may be able to help you get on track. Or, you can go to the writing center and ask to work with someone on this project. Meet with that person a couple of times a week. The tutor might even be willing to go to the library with you or sit at a computer terminal with you and help you find sources.

If you've gotten hopelessly behind, go to your instructor and see if you can make a deal, perhaps taking an incomplete in the course and finishing the paper over the break. Explain how you got in this fix and say that you don't want to cheat.

Finally, if taking an incomplete is not possible, you can "take the hit" for your lapse as a student. Tell your instructor that you are dropping out of the course, and why. Take the *F* and come back and repeat the course. It'll be easier the second time around. At most institutions, your new grade will replace the old in your permanent record. Years later you'll feel good about your decision.

Appendix

How to Pass a Timed Writing Test

Timed writing tests are used to measure your general writing ability or your ability to write a particular kind of essay. Such tests require you to produce an essay within a limited period of time, usually one or two hours, in response to a prompt. You will write the essay in a monitored room, such as a university hall or a classroom, not at home.

Unless you are extremely confident about your chances of doing well, you should prepare for taking these exams, since the outcome will have an important effect on your academic career. This appendix offers advice on how to do well on such tests. You can improve your chances by preparing for the specific type of timed test that you will take and by understanding how the graders assess timed essays.

Timed essays can be categorized by their purposes and by the different kinds of prompts that they use. The next two sections describe the various types of timed writing tests.

A-1 Purposes

Your college or your instructor may require you and your fellow students to take a timed writing test for any of these five purposes:

1. to place students in the appropriate composition course (the regular course or a preparatory course)
2. to exempt talented students from composition requirements

3. to get a writing sample from each student to gauge initial ability

4. to get a paper from each student for grading purposes in a course

5. to maintain standards for the composition program or the university system (this would be an "exit test").

Timed essays are also used to provide the English department with data for composition research, or for evaluation of the department's composition program, but in those cases the essays will be anonymous and your academic career will not be affected. Let's look at each of the five purposes that do affect you.

1. Placement

If the composition program at your college includes a "basic" (remedial) writing course for weak writers, or any other kind of preparatory course (such as a grammar course), the school needs to know how to identify those students who belong in that course. Some do it by looking at SAT or ACT Verbal scores. Most, however, require entering students to take a writing placement test.

Before taking a placement test, you should decide whether or not you want to pass it. If you see yourself as a weak writer who needs as much help as possible, then you don't have to worry about the placement test. You can happily flunk it and get placed in a preparatory course. And if you accidentally pass it, you will undoubtedly be allowed to start with a preparatory course anyway, if that's your wish. Likewise, if you don't have any sense of how good a writer you are relative to your fellow students, you may want the test to determine if you should take a preparatory course. And finally, if you are a good writer, you will probably do well on the test (though there's an outside chance that you won't).

If you are not sure you are going to pass and you don't want to take a preparatory course, then you should follow the advice in this appendix on beating the test. There are good reasons for not wanting to take remedial or pre-composition courses. First, even though the remedial credits count towards being fully registered so that you can play on a sports team or receive loans, those credits (called "institutional credits") usually don't count toward graduation. In other words, if it takes a minimum of 130 credits to graduate, and you take a 3-credit remedial course, then you will have to take a total of 133 credits to graduate.

Another reason for not wanting to take a preparatory course is that it delays your progress through the composition program. That may mean, for example, putting off learning to write the library/Internet research paper. You may find yourself having to write such a paper early in your academic career, perhaps even in the first year, for an introductory course in a non-English subject, such as philosophy or history or psychology. If you don't think you need a preparatory course—why suffer the delay?

Is it ethical to "beat the test"? Yes. If you are confident that you can do OK in the regular composition course, and you are sophisticated enough to use the information below to get a passing grade on the placement test, then you deserve the chance to start out in the regular composition course.

2. Exemption

If you do particularly well on the placement test, you may be excused from one or more composition courses. It may also be possible to get exempted from the first regular composition through the College-Level Examination Program (CLEP). The obvious advantage of skipping a course is that you will move through the composition program faster.

The disadvantage of skipping the first *regular* (non-remedial) composition course is that you will probably miss out on some useful analyses of academic writing, and you will certainly miss out on whatever practice and critiques the course offers.

3. Writing Samples

An instructor might want an in-class writing sample early in the term to get a feel for how well the class as a whole writes.

Such samples are frequently kept on file as a record of each student's initial level of development, in case the student starts to hand in essays that look professionally written (that is, stolen). The instructor can then pull out the in-class sample and argue that "the person who wrote the weak prose in this in-class essay could not possibly have produced this out-of-class essay, except by cheating."

This anti-cheating purpose is sometimes extended into portfolio evaluation. Kansas State University, for example, asks students to submit an end-of-the-term portfolio of their papers written outside of class, to be evaluated by a composition teacher other than the student's. However, one of the papers in the folder must be an essay written in class, so that a sense of the student's initial ability can be gauged. Then, if drafts of the out-of-class essays show "unexplained leaps in progress," the reader might give the portfolio an F.

4. Course Paper

Some instructors simply ask students to write compositions in class. This turns ordinary paper assignments into timed writing tests.

5. Standards

Some English departments require students to write a satisfactory timed essay in order to get credit for a composition course. The purpose of such a policy is to assure the department that students will not be passed on by an instructor who is an easy grader, but instead will be able to write at a satisfactory level.

Besides the English department, the college itself, or the state university system, may set a standard for writing. Students in the California state system, for example, must pass a writing test to become sophomores. In Florida, students cannot matriculate to the junior year, or transfer from a community college to a state university, unless they have passed the state's writing test. Students in the Georgia state system have to pass the "Regents Testing Program," which includes a timed essay, in order to graduate from college. They begin taking the writing test in the freshman year and can take it every semester thereafter until they pass. Those who haven't passed it by the junior year must take a special composition course on writing timed essays.

Obviously, passing an "exit test" is crucial to progressing smoothly through college.

Timed essays have been rightly criticized as crude measures of writing ability. In fact, Kansas State University justifies its portfolio exit assessment on that basis:

> We believe that timed final examinations do not do justice to the way most people write. Most people need time in order to write well. They need time to brainstorm and organize ideas, time to write a rough draft, and time to ask friends and experts for advice about how they might revise their rough drafts. You cannot do this in a two-hour final examination. . . . The portfolio exam shows what you can do much more accurately than a single, timed final exam.

Be that as it may, timed essays are everywhere, even within the Kansas State portfolio requirement (one paper in the portfolio has to be an in-class essay). You will very likely have to write a high-stakes in-class essay at some point in your college career.

A-2 Prompts

You will never be asked to write a timed essay on any subject you feel like writing on. Instead, you will always be given a specific question or statement—called a prompt—to write in response to. There are three general kinds of prompts:

1. **A personal question** that asks you to write about your
   life. For example, the Georgia Regents exit exam has
   used this question: What was the most important moment of
   your life? Explain. This kind of prompt sometimes uses
   a quotation as the starting point for your essay. The
   University of Hawaii, Manoa, offers this example:
   Wendell Phillips once stated, "What is defeat? Nothing but
   education, nothing but the first step to something better." Think
   of your own defeats and decide if you have learned any lessons
   from them. Drawing on these reflections, write an essay in
   which you describe and defend your position.

2. **A social question** that asks you to bring to bear your
   knowledge and reading to answer a question about
   contemporary American life. Here's an example,
   again from the Georgia Regents writing test: Do you
   think smoking should be banned in public areas? Why?

3. **A response to an essay** or a short passage. In 1987,
   The California University system, for example, gave
   students an essay by anthropologist Clyde Kluckhohn and asked them to write in response to this
   prompt: How does Kluckhohn explain the differences and
   similarities among the world's peoples? What do you think
   about his views? Use examples from your own experience,
   reading or observation in developing your essay.

   The rest of this appendix looks at strategies for passing
timed writing tests. Boxes A-1 and A-2 provide prompts for
practice.

Box A-1 An Essay Prompt for Practice

Prompt: Write an essay which briefly summarizes Willa North's essay and responds to North, indicating the points on which you agree and disagree with her. Defend your viewpoint.

The Ideal School System
by
Willa North

One thing all critics of modern American education seem to agree on is that things are worse than they used to be. Students seem not only to learn less but to be less interested in learning. The atmosphere of our high schools has deteriorated: hoodlums stalk the hallways, drugs are everywhere, even the average decent kid dresses like a bum and probably has a social disease. How did we arrive at such a state?

I believe that one of our major mistakes of the last several decades has been to try to educate too many people. It is that overcrowding that makes things worse. The problems of discipline and drugs and general apathy in high schools arise largely from the boredom of students who have no interest whatsoever in academic matters. They are merely putting in their time, and while they do so they disrupt the educational process for other students. Let's get rid of them. Though each child may deserve a chance at formal education, I don't believe that the government, or you the tax payer, has the obligation to educate anyone past puberty if the person by that time shows no ability and no interest.

How should we go about weeding out those who waste teachers' time and those who disrupt the work of their fellow students? I offer a simple and painless answer. We merely adopt the European and Japanese method of allowing students to advance through various stages of education on the basis of examinations. I wouldn't establish a system quite as demanding as some that exist elsewhere. In Japan, for example, students

continued

Box A-1 An Essay Prompt for Practice *continued*

commit suicide under the pressures of such examinations. But in that country, entrance to a top university assures one's future, and the competition is fierce for those few opportunities. In the United States, we may want to educate a larger percentage of our youth on the university level than the Japanese or Europeans. Still, we don't need to educate nearly as many as we now do.

I suggest a national examination for students wishing to enter high school. This would make the atmosphere of junior high a lot more serious, since students would know that in order to stay in school beyond 9th grade they would have to learn a few things. As matters stand now, peer pressure for 9th graders is in the direction of goofing off. Under the new system, the pressure might be to buckle down and study in order to continue on to high school with all one's friends. Let's say that this exam is set up so that about 60 percent of the students will pass it.

Already the situation in high school is far better. Much of the discipline problem and much of the tedious drain on the teachers' time and energy (for remedial work) will have been headed off by the rejection of the 40 percent who didn't pass the entrance exam.

Just to keep the high schoolers on their toes, I recommend a second national exam, one which students would have to pass in order to receive a high school degree. I suggest that this test be composed in such a way that, once again, 40 percent fail it. In other words, of the 60 percent who went on to high school, only 60 percent of them would graduate. If we started with a 100 students, 60 would go to high school; 36 would graduate. If half of the 36 went to college, that would be 18, or 18 percent of the original 100. If that percentage were deemed too low, the national exams could always be adjusted.

On the public school level, I don't think anything more is needed than to get rid of the bad elements and put some pressure on the good elements among the student population. That would solve all our major problems and would turn education in this country around.

Box A-2 Personal and Social Prompts for Practice

Some Prompts That Ask Personal Questions:

1. Describe a person who has had a strong effect on your life. Explain how and why.

2. Describe an important event in your life that taught you something. What did you learn?

3. What are your strongest and weakest qualities? How do you know? What do you need to do to overcome your weaknesses?

Some Prompts That Ask Social Questions:

1. If you became the principal of the high school you graduated from, what would you change and why?

2. The gangster Al Capone once told a crowd of newspaper reporters:

> I make my money by supplying a public demand. If I break the law, my customers, who number hundreds of the best people in Chicago, are as guilty as I am. The only difference between us is that I sell and they buy. Everybody calls me a racketeer. I call myself a business man. When I sell liquor, it's bootleging. When my patrons serve it on a silver tray on Lake Shore Drive, it's hospitality.

What social problem is Mr. Capone pointing out? What is the solution?

3. When foreigners look at Americans, some of them see a people who are overweight, or a people who are too powerful and bullying, or a people who use up too much of the world's natural resources. Should we "trim down"? Where should we trim, why, and how? Or if not, why not?

A-3 Analyze the Prompt

No matter how well written your essay is, if it fails to pro-vide what the prompt asks for, it won't get a passing grade. Even an imbalanced answer, in which you focus almost entirely on one question in the prompt and say very little in response to others, will probably earn a failing grade. It is crucial, therefore, to analyze the prompt.

To begin, underline key words that

1. ask you to do things, such as <u>contrast</u>, <u>explain why</u>, <u>define</u>, <u>give examples</u>
2. name the topic or otherwise limit what you are to talk about.

Let's analyze some prompts, beginning with a personal essay prompt:

How is your <u>life different today</u> from what it was like <u>a year ago</u>?

The topic is your *life.* The key action lies in the adjective *different,* which tells you to *contrast* two things, to show differ-ences. This is a restriction on what you can talk about regarding your life. The words *today* and *a year ago* further restrict the contrast to those periods.

If you start to show similarities in your life between those periods, you are moving off the track. If you start to discuss any aspect of your life a year ago that is not contrasted with your life today, you are moving off the track. If you start to discuss any aspect of your life today that you will not eventu-ally contrast with your life a year ago, you are moving off the track. Spend too much time off the track and the reader will conclude that you are not responding to the prompt.

Here's a social essay prompt:

<u>Americans</u> are said to pride themselves on being a <u>generous</u> people—how is that <u>true</u>, <u>and</u> how is it <u>false</u>?

In responding to this prompt, you will be moving off the track if you talk a lot about other peoples (non-Americans) or discuss at length any other aspect of the American character besides generosity (or its opposite, a lack of generosity). You will also fail to respond to the prompt if you fail to discuss how this generalization about Americans is true, or if you fail to discuss how it is false. You must do both. That's why you would want to underline the key word *and* in the prompt.

Here's an essay-response prompt:

> <u>Discuss</u> what <u>you think</u> are the <u>most important points</u> Dr. Martin Luther <u>King makes</u> in his "I Have a Dream" speech. [The speech would be provided as part of the prompt.]

At the beginning, the vague word *discuss* is not very helpful, except that it doesn't limit what you can say, as words like *contrast, explain* and *define* do. The topic is clearly "the most important points that Dr. Martin Luther King makes." So one thing you will have to do is identify those points during your reading and planning stage. While reading the speech, you would underline potential points for discussion; then during planning you would make your decision as to which ones to go with.

The last underlined phrase, *King makes*, reminds you not to go off on a tangent talking about what others have said about civil rights. Stick to King.

In such an essay, of course, you are expressing your opinion as to which of the points King makes are important. In fact, the phrase <u>you think</u> appears in the prompt, and you would be smart to underline it. You should always back up opinions in a timed essay. It is not enough to simply identify and explain the meaning of King's strongest points, you should also defend those choices, defend your opinion, by answering the question of *why you think* each point is important.

For example, early in the speech, King says that the Constitution promises basic rights to all "men," not just white men. An explanation of that point might assert that since the promise is to all men, it includes blacks. That's the meaning of the point. Now, why do *you* see it as significant? You could argue that you see this as an important point (1) because it rejects the old racist notion that blacks are not "men" (humans), (2) because violations of our Constitution are always serious, and (3) because this promise comes from that part of the Constitution that addresses the most basic principles that define our nation. Those would be your reasons for selecting this point as important.

A-4 Think and Plan before Writing

Under the pressure of a test, it is easy to start writing gibberish or to immediately go off on a tangent and not know how to get back. You end up crossing out big sections at the beginning, a sure sign to readers that you failed to organize your thoughts before writing. That lowers the readers' expectations for your essay, and readers tend to find what they expect.

Never try to write a timed essay off the top of your head, without thinking and planning.

If you've got an hour for your essay, spend twenty minutes planning. Planning is writing—it's not a waste of valuable time. List main points, leaving room to note how they might be developed. Create as full an outline as you can. Work on your outline—change, delete, and add ideas. Once you know pretty much what you are going to say, a half an hour is plenty of time to write three to five pages in the exam booklet.*

The numbered steps below provide an effective procedure. The procedure may look complicated, but you can learn it by using it while writing a practice essay in preparation for the test.

---

* The exam booklet, sometimes called a "blue book" because of the blue cover, is what you will probably write your essay in; bluebooks are usually handed out along with the prompt, but you may be asked to buy one at the campus bookstore and bring it with you to the test.

1. **Read and study the prompt, underlining the key words.**

   If responding to an essay prompt, you should also:
   a. Read the essay looking for passages that seem to address the prompt; mark those passages.
   b. Put a "Q" in the margin next to lines you may want to quote.
   c. Reread the marked passages to get a summary of the essay in your head.
   d. Reread the prompt.

2. **Write up your outline**, your list of points in the order you will make them. Do all your planning at the back of the exam booklet, or clearly mark planning material as such, so that your outline and warm up statements aren't confused with your actual essay.

3. **Write the essay using every other line**, so you can neatly make changes and additions as you read over your finished essay.

4. **Put a title on your essay** once it is finished and you know what it ultimately says about the topic.

5. **Proofread** your essay for spelling errors, missing words or word endings, poor phrasing, and other problems you are capable of recognizing.

A-5 Write a Highly Structured Essay

Student essays written under exam pressure tend not to be well organized. The pre-structured essay (described in Chapter 1 and illustrated in Box 1-1) has the advantage of presenting an obvious, unmistakable organization. Your first job in writing a pre-structured essay is to create a thesis—the main point you are going to make in the essay—and to write down that thesis in a sentence or two. For example:

> —Martin Luther King makes three important points in his "I Have a Dream" speech.

—Americans are both generous and selfish, depending on the
situation.
—James Conant exaggerates the degree to which sports under-
mine academics in our schools.

The best place for the thesis statement is at the end of
the first paragraph. That means you're going to have to write
several sentences that lead up to that conclusion. For the
King essay, you could introduce King as an important figure
and his speech as his most important, long-lasting statement.
This may seem like empty-headed blather, but that's OK.
This kind of gentle leading up to the thesis is accepted ritual.

The use of a numeral ("three") in your thesis sentence
for the King essay sets up the organization for the rest of the
paper. You will discuss each of the three important points
King makes. To do so, first you will state (or quote) the point
and explain what it means. Then you will explain why you
think it is so important. That will take one or two paragraphs.
Then you move on to the next point, and so forth. Your concluding paragraph will quickly restate the three points and
make a generalization about their importance: These ideas
will remain an important part of Dr. Martin Luther King's legacy. Again,
the statement doesn't really say anything profound, but no
matter; it is a conventional "sign off" or "bowing out"—a way
of smoothly exiting the essay.

This simplistic canned structure may not earn you a
good grade for an out-of-class assignment, but in the chaotic
world of timed writing, a tidy essay shines like a new nickel in
a spray of old pennies.

For the "Americans" essay, you could start with the idea
that Americans are often said to be generous, but they are
also often described as selfish. So you ask, in your first paragraph: Which is the truth? You would then claim that neither
statement is completely true, because "the reality is more
complicated." That's safe to say, because the reality is always
more complicated than any one viewpoint suggests. Now you
are ready to present your thesis sentence: Americans are both

generous and selfish, depending on the situation. The organization of such an essay is self-evident. First you would state the situations under which Americans are generous, and then you would do the same for selfish. Be sure to follow the order set up in your thesis sentence. If that sentence says "generous and selfish," discuss generous first.

After your opening paragraph is at least planned, if not written, your next step is to create topic sentences for each of the paragraphs in the body of the essay. The outline below does that:

> THESIS: Americans are generous or selfish depending on the circumstances.

1. American can be a generous people.
   —my home town story: generous response to a boy whose parents were killed
   —helping Bosnians from being wiped out
2. However, Americans can be selfish.
   —parents selfish about schools, moving to districts with good schools for their kids instead of helping to improve poor schools
   —U.S. gives smaller percentage of foreign aid compared to Europe and Japan
3. Explanation is that Americans like to see their generosity pay off quickly
   —will help a person out of a jam, but less interested in long term efforts to help a group, such as poor children going to poor schools
   —like to act decisively to help a nation or people in immediate trouble, but less interested in long term efforts like foreign aid, which may not even be effective

A-6 Write a Classic Argument

Besides the pre-structured essay, you can also choose the classic argument structure if you are asked to agree or disagree with an author whose essay is part of the prompt.

The Conant essay on sports in our schools can be handled with the methods of argumentation discussed in chapter 8.

At the beginning of any timed essay that responds to an essay prompt, introduce the title and the author:

> James Conant, in his essay "Athletics: The Poison Ivy in Our Schools," says that we overemphasize school sports and that academics suffer as a result.

For the rest of the first paragraph, continue to review the essay broadly, ending with your reaction in the form of a thesis statement:

> Conant feels that we may lose our competition with the rest of the world if we don't concentrate more on academics. I agree that there may be some degree of overemphasis on sports, but Conant exaggerates the problem.

Following the approach to argumentation discussed in Chapter 8, present arguments from Conant's essay and then refute those arguments. You might start by making a small concession to Conant's logic, before turning away to state your own:

> I agree that parents sometimes get overly enthusiastic about sporting events. However, when it comes to schools, parents are not just interested in sports. They are also interested in the quality of education that the school is providing.

Then move on to the next point that Conant makes that constitutes an exaggeration of a problem. Repeat the pattern for several points and you're done with this part of the essay.

Next, present your own view or solution, beginning with a topic sentence: The real academic problem in our schools lies in the boring way subjects are traditionally taught. At this stage, you can safely abandon further discussion of the prompt's essay and focus entirely on your own views on the subject. Once you have paid your due respect to the prompt essay, graders like to see you take off on your own and show some creative thinking on the issue under discussion.

A-7 Avoid Obvious Signs of Incompetence

The faculty who read and evaluate placement and exit essays have one of the most boring jobs every created. They sit amidst huge stacks of hundreds, even thousands, of unimpressive, handwritten essays, every one on the same topic. This is not the fault of the students taking the test. The conditions of the test—a timed essay on a surprise topic with no opportunity for deep thought or serious revision—guarantee that few participants will write an essay that is truly interesting.

The readers have to assign a grade to each essay, distinguishing between one dull effort and another. A typical scale is 1-4, with 1 or 2 as failing grades, 3 and 4 as passing grades. The few essays in the 1 category and the 4 category stand out from the rest, but it isn't always easy to distinguish between a 2 essay and a 3 essay. Most grades will be 2's and 3's. So for hundreds of essays, the evaluator must puzzle out which grade to give, a 2 (meaning the student takes the remedial course or fails the exit test) or a 3 (meaning the student begins the composition sequence with the regular course or passes the exit test).

Inevitably, many readers take shortcuts. They find ways to recognize failing essays without reading them carefully or completely. For example, any essay that is particularly short is almost certain to be badly written and underdeveloped. The student who writes only half a page in an exam booklet instead of the usual three or four is probably someone who doesn't know how to develop any kind of essay, much less respond to the prompt. So the reader reads the first few sentences, to make sure that the student isn't a terrifically talented writer who can say a lot in a few words, then pastes a 1 or 2 on it and shoves it into the flunk pile.

An essay with no paragraph indentations will end up there, too.

Extremely bad handwriting suggests incompetence. It is often the mark of a student awkward at school things, like writing. And even if the essay has some merit, the reader may not be able to decipher enough text to appreciate the talent that lies beneath the scrawl. Harried, bored, and irritable readers tend to give such essays the ax without struggling to decipher them. Likewise, big loopy handwriting with curlicues (known as "sorority style" by cynical test readers), though fairly easy to read, gives the impression of airheadedness. Airheads belong in Remedial Writing and don't deserve to pass exit tests.

So to beat the test, write an essay of at least medium length, in clear unadorned handwriting. If your handwriting is awful, learn to print fast.

A-8 Avoid Fatal Errors

Rightly or wrongly, many professionals in English perceive certain sentence errors as the mark of an undeveloped writer who belongs in the remedial course or who doesn't deserve to pass the exit test. Here are some of those fatal errors that show up in test essays:

—Using the wrong homophone (in particular, confusing *its* and *it's*, *to* and *too*, or *there* and *their*). Learn the three pairs just listed.

—Misspelling *where* (students leave out the *h* and write *were*)

—Writing *of* instead of *have* in a verb phrase: He could of done better, instead of the correct He could have done better

—Writing a possessive as a plural: By the years end. . . ., instead of the correct By the year's end. . . . You can get away with this

kind of error once, but if you repeat it, the grader will conclude that you don't know this basic fact about the English
language. If you don't understand this grammatical point,
before the test, look up "apostrophe" in your handbook and
study its use in forming "possessives."

—Putting a comma after (instead of before) *and, but,* or *or*
when they are connecting two complete sentences: He fought
hard but, he didn't win, instead of the correct He fought hard, but he
didn't win.

—Putting a comma between two sentences with no *and, but,*
or *or*; the infamous "comma splice":

> Conant opposes our obsession with sports at the high school level,
> he thinks it distorts the purpose of school.

A semicolon (;) is the appropriate punctuation after *level.* Or
a period, starting a new sentence with He thinks. . . .
   You can probably get away with one comma splice, but
two suggests that the mistakes are errors of ignorance, not
slip ups under pressure. Some English faculty believe that a
student who writes run-together sentences "doesn't know
what a sentence is." That conclusion has fatal consequences.

—Referring to an author by his or her first name and vaguely
referring to works without naming their titles:

> In his article, Jeff thinks that our education system is improving.

Here's how to do it correctly:

> In "What Isn't Wrong with Reading," Jeff McQuillan argues that our
> schools are improving.

See Chapter 5 for more on this subject.

Certain other very common word errors may not be fatal, but they make you look dumb, which doesn't help your chances for success. For example:

—Misuse of the word *emphasize.* Some students wrongly use *emphasize* when all they really mean is something like "believes" or "says":

> Conant emphasizes that sports can be bad.

No, Conant <u>says</u> that sports can be bad, or he <u>believes</u> that sports can be bad.

—Misuse of the word *believe.* Don't write,

> In his essay, Conant believes that sports are overemphasized.

People believe things in their heads, not in their essays. In their essays, they <u>say</u> things or <u>write</u> things:

> In his essay, Conant says that sports are overemphasized.

Or you can simply say that Conant believes something, without putting "in his essay" in front of that statement:

> Conant believes that sports are overemphasized.

—Misuse of the word *society.* Avoid this vague use of the word:

> In society today, we overemphasize sports.

Write something like this:

> Contemporary American culture overemphasizes sports.

Because the bulk of test essays are unimpressive in content, these surface errors can take on excessive importance. Many readers look for an unmistakable sign of ignorance that will allow them to make an easy decision when they have finished reading the essay, or even to stop reading the essay and toss it in the flunk pile. So part of your strategy for beating the test should be to keep an eye out for such fatal errors when you proofread.

A-9 Avoid Emotional, Exaggerated Statements

As Chapter 4 discusses in detail, an educated tone is quiet and calm, projecting a polite, reasonable, logical person behind the words. Don't use insulting language or overstate your claims:

> Conant is really dumb about sports. When he was in school, he probably warmed the bench for the ping pong team! There's nothing wrong with sports in schools.

This sounds more educated:

> We shouldn't let sports undermine academics in our schools, but the problem is not as bad as Conant thinks.

A-10 Leave Your Extremist Views at the Test Room Door

If you believe that private citizens should be allowed to own hand-held missile launchers with nuclear warheads to protect themselves from the federal government, or that President Bush is actually Satan, don't mention those opinions in your essay. Focus instead on widely held views that you agree with. Say that "private citizens should be allowed to arm themselves sufficiently to help repel an attack on our country, should it ever come" or that "Bush is leading our country to economic and environmental disaster." Those are strong enough statements. Anything much stronger, and the reader will start wondering if you belong in college or on an FBI suspect list.

A-11 Add Sparks of Intelligence

The sudden, proper use of a semicolon will jump off the page at the reader like a beacon from outer space announcing the existence of intelligent life. So sprinkle your essay with such signs. Here are some possibilities:

—**Use a semicolon** (;). Instead of starting a new sentence closely related to the previous one, attach it with a semicolon:

> Test readers are influenced by signs of ignorance; they are also impressed by signs of intelligence.

—**Use a colon** (:) after a noun to set up a list:

> My life is different from six months ago in three ways: I've gone from saying goodbye to long-time friends to making new friends, I've gone from living with my parents to living in a dorm with a room-mate, and I've gone from half-heartedly studying general subjects to seriously studying for my professional career in accounting.

Make sure you are putting the colon after a noun (*ways* in the above sentence) and not a verb or a preposition, as in these sentences:

> To improve reading, McQuillan advocates: more access to print materials, better teaching methods, and better assessment.

> To improve reading, McQuillan argues for:
> -more access to print materials
> -better teaching methods
> -better assessment.

Professional writers, in fact, do put colons after verbs and prepositions, but English handbooks are critical of that positioning. They want the colon only after nouns. Test readers know the handbook guidelines inside out, and many will see the colon after a verb or preposition as an error—and that will defeat your purpose in using the thing in the first place.

—**Emphasize parallel structure** in a long sentence. Structures are parallel when elements in a list take the same form. Both of these sentences are parallel:

> He likes skiing, hiking, and swimming.
> He likes to ski, to hike, and to swim.

Let's emphasize the parallel structure in the second of those sentences by repeating more words:

> He likes to ski, he likes to hike, and he likes to swim.

Normally, a writer wouldn't bother to make the parallelism so heavy in such a short sentence. Let's take another look at the original sentence illustrating the colon:

> My life is different from six months ago in three ways: I've gone from saying goodbye to long-time friends to making new friends, I've gone from living with my parents to living in a dorm with a room-mate, and I've gone from half-heartedly studying general subjects to seriously studying for my professional career in accounting.

Because this sentence is long, the use of heavy parallelism contributes to clarity. The parallelism is emphasized here through the repetition of *I've gone from.* That model sentence provides a double whammy: proper use of the colon plus heavy parallelism.

—**Use a few sophisticated words**, spelled correctly (don't ruin the effect by misspelling them). Instead of misusing the word *emphasize,* use it correctly, and at the same time, throw in the sophisticated word *de-emphasize*: Conant wants us to de-emphasize sports and emphasize academics.

Put together a list of words you can drop into your essay. Verbs related to thought processes are good choices, since you are likely to find uses for them. When practicing for the test, try writing a paragraph which uses one of these: *critiques, argues (that), denounces, applauds, denigrates, celebrates, perceives, mitigates, reduces, expands, manipulates, marginalizes, synthesizes, opposes, supports, advocates.*

—Quote from the text that appears in the prompt. Suppose the prompt includes Martin Luther King's famous "I Have a Dream" speech, and you are to answer this question in your essay: What are the strongest points that Dr. King makes in this speech? Defend your answer. When you go to name each point, quote from King directly:

> King argues that the Constitution promises freedom and equality to all Americans, but that through segregation, "America has defaulted on this promissory note."

Note how King's words are incorporated smoothly and grammatically into the sentence. Notice also the use of the verb *argues,* one of the words you might bring with you in your head to the test.

—Give your essay a title. A good title incorporates the prompt in some way:

Are Americans Generous?
Martin Luther Kings' Three Big Points
How My Life Has Changed in the Past Year

Don't make a mistake about what words are properly capitalized in a title and what words are not. Use your handbook to learn this kind of information. Do NOT put quotation marks around your own title at the top of the first page. Do put them around the titles of other people's articles, book chapters, or essays that you mention in your essay. If you happen to mention a book that you've read or a movie you've seen, underline the title (underlining is a substitute for italics). The titles of short works require quotation marks around them; the titles of long works should be underlined.

A-12 Mention a Literary Text That You Have Read

English teachers like to see people use literature as a way of understanding the complexities of life. Show that you can do that. Before the test, review a play or novel or short story or poem by a famous writer that you have read. Then try to work in a reference to that work in your essay. Here's an opening paragraph for a response to the prompt-question How is your life different today from what it was like a year ago?

> Like Billy Pilgrim in Vonnegut's novel *Slaughterhouse Five*, I felt "unstuck in time" when our family moved back to our hometown in Indiana after three years in Palm Beach, Florida. Would my old mall rat friends still be haunting the Palace Mall? Would people I had known look the same? A year ago, I was enjoying sunny beaches. Would the snow kill me? Would I be happy?

Here's another example:

> My parents got divorced last year. Because I was 17, they let me decide which parent I would live with. Like the traveler in Robert Frost's poem "Stopping by Woods on a Snowy Evening," I had to make a big life decision. Should I live with my stable, reliable mother or my unstable but always interesting father? I knew that the rest of my life would be different depending on which path I took.

A-13 What If You Fail the Test?

If it's an exit test, find out when you can take it again, and this time *prepare!* Or prepare *more!* Though the prompt will be different next time, it will be the same type. Use the practice prompts in Boxes A-1 and A-2, or invent your own, and practice writing essays in response, allowing yourself the amount of time that's available for the real test. You might get your efforts reviewed at the writing center, to see how they could have been written better.

If it's a placement test and you really feel that you don't need any remedial work, ask if you can retake the test right away. English faculty understand that a single performance on a timed writing test may not accurately reflect your writing ability, especially if you were nervous, or were feeling ill, or were thrown by the prompt. If you say that you are certain that you can pass if given a second opportunity, the department might give you that chance.

If things don't work out and you end up in a preparatory course that you wish you didn't have to take, don't go into the course in a sullen frame of mind, resistant to learning. That only hurts you further. Go into the course determined to get an A and learn as much as possible. That's your best revenge on the system.

If you fail an exit test, even more than once, don't despair. Don't quit college. Don't let this test stop you from becoming an educated person. Keep on preparing and retaking it. There's a luck element here that will eventually work to your favor. Sooner or later you'll get a prompt that you can easily write on, or you'll get a reader who likes the way you think and gives you a passing grade. Think of this test as an irritating, temporary hurdle, not a permanent obstruction. Just do the work to get past it, and then you can forget about it for the rest of your life.

Index